CPSM® Study Guide

2nd edition

Effective Supply Management Performance (Exam 2)

Editor: Robert B. Handfield, Ph.D. (2008)

Revised by: Linda L. Stanley, Ph.D. (2014)

Contributing Editors:

Holly LaCroix Johnson

Scott R. Sturzl, CPSM, CPSD

Terri Tracey, CAE

ISM® Certified Professional in Supply Management® Program
Published by:
Institute for Supply Management®

institute for
supply management

©2014 All rights reserved.
Institute for Supply Management® (ISM®)
2055 East Centennial Circle
Tempe, Arizona 85284
USA

www.ism.ws

Table of Contents

Product and Service Development

Project Management

Quality

Index

Purpose of the Study Guide

The CPSM® *Study Guide* offers an overview of the material covered in the Examination. The information contained in the Guide is meant to provide the exam candidate with an introduction to the major components covered in the test, and to provide direction for additional study. The Guide is constructed according to the CPSM® Exam Specifications and is divided into three exams: Exam 1, Exam 2 and Exam 3.

The CPSM® *Study Guide* takes a step-by-step approach to the basic material covered in the Exam Specifications and lists the major parts of the exam, followed by the task and the knowledge, skill and ability areas (KSAs) related to each task.

While the *Study Guide* provides a summary of the type of content covered on the exam, the candidate should recognize that the *Study Guide* is not meant to serve as a substitute for any of the major textbooks in the field of supply management. ISM lists supplemental study materials including the ISM *Professional Series* on its website, www.ism.ws. The ISM *Professional Series* is a three-book series that covers content included in the Exam. Candidates are strongly urged to use at least one of the major supply management texts in addition to the *Study Guide* when preparing for the Exam. Reading the Study Guide alone, without any other resources, is not considered to be sufficient preparation for the Exam. Also, please be aware that the actual exam may contain material that may not be covered in the *Study Guide*.

The CPSM® *Study Guide* (2008) was the work of several talented individuals in the field of supply management, who have graciously offered their time and expertise to this project. This revised edition is based on the revised CPSM® specifications (2013) and the work of Linda L. Stanley, Ph.D., Faculty Associate in the W.P. Carey School of Business at Arizona State University and Adjunct Professor at Thunderbird School of Global Management. Assistant Professor of Supply Chain Management, Michigan State University, Supply Chain Management Department. The Institute for Supply Management (ISM) is grateful for their professionalism and sincere desire to see this project successfully completed.

Exam 2 Contributors — Effective Supply Management Performance

Jill B. Bossi, C.P.M., Vice President & Chief Procurement Officer American Red Cross

Stephen Chapman, Ph.D., Associate Professor, North Carolina State University, College of Management

S. Tom Foster, Ph.D., Area Leader and Professor of Supply Chain Management, Brigham Young University

Eric Haft, Global Ombudsman, IBM

Robert B. Handfield, Ph.D., Bank of America Distinguished Professor of Supply Chain Management, North Carolina State University, Department of Business Management

Larry B. Kroeger, Program Director, ISC University Relations and Supply Chain Leadership Program

Benn Lawson, Senior Lecturer in Operations Management, University of Cambridge; Director of the Centre for Process Excellence and Innovation (CPEI)

Rene G. Rendon, DBA, C.P.M., Professor, Naval Postgraduate School

Sue Perrott Siford, Ph.D., CMA, Professor Emerita, Arizona State University

Linda L. Stanley, Ph.D., Faculty Associate, W.P. Carey School of Business, Arizona State University; Adjunct Professor, Thunderbird School of Global Management

David Van Valkenburgh, CPSM, C.P.M., A.P.P., Consumer Materials Manager, Cummins Power Generation – Fridley

Contributing Editors

Holly LaCroix Johnson

Scott Sturzl, CPSM, C.P.M., A.P.P.

Terri Tracey, CAE

ISM also wishes to recognize and thank all of the editors and contributors to the various editions of the C.P.M. *Study Guide* for the excerpts taken from their work.

Introduction

The Institute for Supply Management (ISM) is the first supply management institute in the world and one of the most respected. Founded in 1915, ISM's mission is to enhance the value and performance of procurement and supply chain management practitioners and their organizations worldwide. ISM is a not-for-profit institute that provides opportunities for the promotion of the profession and the expansion of professional skills and knowledge.

With its mission in mind, in 2008 ISM undertook an enormous task by developing a new professional certification program with a comprehensive Exam Specification for the ISM procurement and supply management body of knowledge. ISM recognizes that changes in the field demand that the new program reflect the skills necessary for both today and tomorrow for a supply management professional. The CPSM® program addresses the realities of supply management, as well as workplace complexities including globalization, use of technology and expanded competencies that procurement and supply management professionals employ to drive value in their organizations. This Exam Specification was updated in 2013, and the ISM *Study Guide* was updated to include this new and revised content.

Definition of Supply Management

ISM defines supply management as the identification, acquisition, access, positioning, management of resources and related capabilities an organization needs or potentially needs in the attainment of its strategic objectives.

Components included under the supply management umbrella include the following list; however, as the scope of supply management professionals shifts, other components may be added.

- Disposition/Investment Recovery

- Distribution

- Inventory Control

- Logistics

- Materials Management

- Operations

- Packaging

- Product/Service Development

- Purchasing/Procurement

- Quality

- Receiving

- Strategic Sourcing

- Transportation/Traffic/Shipping

- Warehousing.

Purpose of the Examination

The Examination is a criterion-referenced occupational test, designed to determine if a candidate is qualified to attain the title of Certified Professional in Supply Management® (CPSM®). To be eligible, one of the requirements is that the candidate must pass Exams 1 through 3 of the examination, or if a current C.P.M. in good standing, pass the Bridge Exam.

Definition of a Supply Management Professional

What exactly is a supply management professional? What sort of job responsibilities and duties distinguish a person in this position? While the actual duties of personnel will vary from organization to organization, ISM has developed the following general definition of the supply management position, which directly reflects the content of the Examination:

> A supply management professional is an individual who provides leadership by aligning resources to define and satisfy diverse internal and external customer needs through the acquisition and ongoing management of goods and services.

The three exams of the examination have been designed to cover the job responsibilities, duties and skills of the individual depicted above.

Content of the Examination

The content of the Examination is based on the findings of a job analysis of the supply management professional position. The test specifications were drawn to reflect the results of this job analysis as thoroughly and as accurately as possible. The examination for Exam 2 includes the following:

Exam 2: Effective Supply Management Performance

    A. Forecasting

    B. Logistics

    C. Materials and Inventory Management

    D. Organization/Departmental Assessment

    E. Planning

    F. Product and Service Development

    G. Project Management

    H. Quality

For an explanation on Important Characteristics of the Examination, please refer to the Introduction section of Exam 1, page xi.

Distributions of Questions Within the Exam

Exam 2: Effective Supply Management Performance

Component Area	Questions	Component Area	Questions
A. Forecasting			
Task 2-A-1	6	Task 2-A-3	6
Task 2-A-2	7		
B. Logistics			
Task 2-B-1	4	Task 2-B-3	5
Task 2-B-2	5	Task 2-B-4	5
C. Materials and Inventory Management.			
Task 2-C-1	6	Task 2-C-3	4
Task 2-C-2	4	Task 2-C-4	5
D. Organization/Department Assessment			
Task 2-D-1	7	Task 2-D-3	7
Task 2-D-2	6	Task 2-D-4	6
E. Planning			
Task 2-E-1	8	Task 2-E-2	7
F. Product and Service Development			
Task 2-F-1	6	Task 2-F-2	6
G. Project Management			
Task 2-G-1	9	Task 2-G-2	10
H. Quality			
Task 2-H-1	6	Task 2-H-3	7
Task 2-H-2	8		
	Total Questions	150 (plus 15 unscored try-out questions)	

Effective Supply Management Performance: Overview of Exam 2

Forecasting

2-A-1   Perform analysis and provide data on current and future and global/domestic market conditions, benchmarks and industry trends to management and/or user departments

2-A-2   Develop supply forecasts in light of economic, competitive, technology, market and currency trends and conditions that affect procurement.

2-A-3   Manage forecasted data with suppliers.

Logistics

2-B-1   Design/modify logistics facility layouts and equipment designs to support business model, increase productivity and lower operating costs.

2-B-2   Direct traffic/distribution policies and procedures to ensure optimum flow of material and consolidation of freight.

2-B-3   Manage international transportation, invoicing and documentation functions to ensure corporate compliance with all governmental import, export, hazardous material and air freight regulations.

2-B-4   Manage the resolution of delivery/receiving problems including freight loss and damage claims.

Materials and Inventory Management

2-C-1   Develop/implement a material and/or service standardization program.

2-C-2   Develop/implement a warehouse and inventory management system.

2-C-3   Coordinate and/or monitor the movement of equipment and assets within the organization.

2-C-4   Develop, oversee and execute multi-channel disposition plan for excess inventory and finished goods.

Organization/ Department Assessment

2-D-1   Monitor work against business plans and take action to resolve variances or adjust plans as appropriate.

2-D-2   Develop performance criteria and evaluate supply management staff performance.

2-D-3 Develop tools and processes to measure, report and improve compliance with supply management policies.

2-D-4 Analyze and resolve issues raised in supply management audit reports.

Planning

2-E-1 Implement or utilize requirements planning (xRP — for example, , Enterprise Resource Planning (ERP), Materials Requirements Planning (MRP), Manufacturing Resource Planning (MRP II), Distribution Requirements Planning (DRP and DRP II), and Warehouse Management Systems (WMS) to align supply management and operations activities to support organizational strategy.) to align supply management and operations activities to support organizational strategy.

2-E-2 Develop, implement, maintain and monitor the forecasting, operations planning, scheduling and inventory control functions to ensure optimum use of capacity and resources.

Product and Service Development

2-F-1 Participate in product/service development or specification/requirement changes that support organizational merchandising and marketing efforts to meet customer needs.

2-F-2 Manage ramp-up strategy and implementation to full-scale production for new product or service introductions.

Project Management

2-G-1 Perform project management activities representing the supply management organization.

2-G-2 Implement a continuous improvement process within the supply chain in accordance with organizational objectives.

Quality

2-H-1 Develop/administer a supplier certification program.

2-H-2 Develop measurements for continuous quality improvement and target setting.

2-H-3 Develop, measure and evaluate quality requirements to continuously improve supplier performance.

Bridge Examination for Current C.P.M.s

The Bridge is an exam for C.P.M.s in good standing who wish to attain the CPSM®. It is a single exam covering contemporary content and material not covered in the current C.P.M. Exam. Candidates may register for the bridge exam through December 31, 2014, and must take the test before December 31, 2015. The bridge exam will not be available after this date. Bridge exam study materials are available, including the prior edition of the *Study Guide*. After passing the Bridge exam, candidates must also meet the non-exam requirements.

Scoring of the Bridge Examination

The scoring of the Bridge examination will be the same as with the CPSM® Examination. Candidates will receive a scaled score ranging between 100 and 600, with the passing score set at 400. Scores received from ISM are reported as scaled scores in increments of 10. If your scaled score on the Bridge Exam is in the range of 100 to 390, you failed the exam. If your scaled score is in the range of 400 to 600, you passed the exam.

Forecasting

Task 2-A-1

Perform analysis and provide data on current and future and global/domestic market conditions, benchmarks and industry trends to management and/or user departments.

1) General issues in economics

Economics is the process by which businesses allocate scarce resources. Trade-offs are an integral part of this equation. Businesses must determine what and how much to produce given restrictions on labor, plant and equipment needs, among many other issues. There are trade-offs between inflation and unemployment rates. Governments play a key role in an economy through regulations, taxes, law enforcement, justice systems, public infrastructure and trade policies.

The world operates with a combination of economic markets. Markets offer varying degrees of competition with price determined primarily by supply and demand.

A) **Industries, firms and markets** — In a centralized economy, price is determined administratively. Even in a free-enterprise capitalistic economy, however, prices sometime bear little relationship to supply and demand. A price can be influenced by market structure or can be set by regulation. Industries and organizations have the freedom to determine what materials they will purchase and what products and services they will produce and sell based on current prices as well as on available supply and demand. Likewise, consumers can freely buy what they want based on price, supply and demand. In reality, no country operates with a pure market economy. In a pure market economy, all labor, goods, services and capital are free from any government restriction or trade barriers so they can move freely across national borders. Most market economies operate with some form of restriction.

Two other types of economies in the world today include the closed economy and the mixed economy. A closed economy is one in which a country severely limits trade with the outside world and relies on its own resources to support production and trade. While there are no completely closed economies in the world today, North Korea and Cuba exhibit many of the traits of a closed economy. Others operate with a mix of state-owned and private enterprises, otherwise known as a mixed economy. Most industrialized nations arguably operate within a mixed economy, including the United States, France and Mexico (Stanley and Matthews 2014).

B) **Global markets** — Global trade is relatively open today. Organizations generally have the ability to market and sell products and services around the world with fewer forms of protectionism than ever. Protectionism according to the ISM *Glossary* (2014) is government interference with the free flow of goods and services that is considered harmful to the domestic economy. Because of lower trade barriers, international competitors have equal access to the least expensive forms of raw materials, labor and technology. As a result, they benefit from similar economies of scale (Stanley and Mathews 2014).

Many nations hold economic advantages in certain commodity areas. Saudi Arabia, for example, has much oil; Canada has timber; Zimbabwe has chrome. Others hold advantages in labor supply, location or climate. An absolute advantage in international trade is said to exist when one of the trading countries can produce a unit of the good involved with less resources than the other, or when only one country has the resources, such as South Africa with natural industrial diamonds.

The natural flow of world trade, reflecting whatever advantages exist, is modified by many factors. Embargoes and quotas can stop or slow the flow of goods, tariffs can wash out price differences, and government subsidies can create an artificial comparative advantage where one does not naturally exist. In some cases this leads to selling a product in other countries at prices below those in the home market. This practice is called "dumping." It is illegal in most importing countries, including the United States (ISM *Glossary* 2014).

C) **Business cycles and trends (for example, lead time)** — The swings in the economy are known as the business cycle.

The business cycle has five phases:

1) The highest point of output before a downturn

2) Recession, or shrinking of the economy

3) Recession trough, or lowest point in economic activity

4) Recovery, or resuming growth path

5) Expansion, beyond previous high point (Stanley and Matthews 2014).

No two business cycles are the same in either intensity or duration. A "recession" leads to a "trough" and a "lower turning point." Expansion (recovery) leads to a "peak" and an "upper turning point." Overlaid on this pattern are long-term economic trends and seasonal variations.

Many things contribute to the cyclical pattern. Political disturbances, wars, population migrations, natural disasters, harvesting conditions and governmental actions in monetary and fiscal policy affect the economy.

Business cycle forecasting models rely on leading indicators such as average hours worked per week, stock prices, construction contract awards and new orders. Some models provide fair estimates of upcoming changes in the output of the domestic economy, usually measured by Gross Domestic Product (GDP). Purchasing and inventory management decisions can be made using this information. Supply management professionals can use this data and indicators to try to forecast the lead time needed in making their decisions.

D) **Transportation trends** — Growth of international trade continues, with an average annual increase of 3.7 percent between 2005 and 2011. As a result, multimodal transportation requirements continue to increase. Logistics service providers and transportation carriers, particularly the airlines, have been growing in size through expansion and acquisition. At the same time, there is a need for better logistical planning for the deployment of multimodal transportation systems and services that effectively move freight because the physical and informational connections between intermodal carriers often is weak.

E) **Economic indicators (for example, ISM *Report On Business*®)** — Understanding economic indicators helps supply management professionals identify those market forces that will affect the supply and demand for a particular commodity, product or service. Leading, lagging and coincident indicators are used to understand the marketplace. (See Task 2-A-2 for a further description of common economic indicators.) ISM's *Report On Business*® is a key economic indicator. There are two reports that cover different sectors of the U.S. economy: Manufacturing and Non-Manufacturing. The indicators measured include: New Orders; Production/Business Activity; Employment; Supplier Deliveries; Inventories; Customers' Inventories (manufacturing report only); Prices; Backlog of Orders; New Export Orders; Imports; and Inventory Sentiment (non-manufacturing report only). The manufacturing report contains the PMI™, which is a composite index based on five of the indexes. The nonmanufacturing report contains the NMI™, which is a composite index based on four of the indexes.

F) **Governmental policies** — Governments are in a unique position to influence economic activity through various means solely at its disposal such as fiscal and monetary policies that, in turn, influence the economic behavior of individuals and organizations. Laws and regulations governing international organizations can change frequently depending on the country. This will add an element of risk to any forecast. It is important for the supply management professional to understand the restrictions and regulations of the governments in which they are doing business so they can plan for the future.

G) **Political stability/instability** — A country or region of the world can be affected economically because of its political stability or instability. The political situation in another country is often a major consideration in doing business with that country. Political factors, either locally or abroad, can affect demand. New administrations, shifts in the political climate and government takeovers are just a few of the changes that may alter an organization's original demand projections.

There is the potential risk of interruptions in supply due to political problems, such as a change in the government leadership or shifts in political sentiment. While the risk is generally higher in lesser developed countries, disruptions can occur anywhere (Stanley and Matthews 2014). An unstable political situation might lead to plant, transportation or port closings, all of which may influence the availability or price of a product or the delivery of a service.

H) **World industrial migration** — Differences in country labor, inflation, interest and currency rates have caused shifts in manufacturing throughout the world. Increasingly, organizations are moving to international sites to tap local markets for low production costs and to establish sales outlets to emerging economies.

I) **Import/export issues** — Free trade versus protectionism. The term "free trade" refers to the uninhibited flow of goods and services across national boundaries (ISM *Glossary* 2014). There are no tariffs, no quotas, and no embargoes on trade. While the term "fair trade" usually implies protectionism, the ISM *Glossary* (2014) defines the term as government interference with the free flow of goods and services that is considered harmful to the domestic economy. An example is quotas on the number of canvas shoes imported into the United States from Korea.

While protectionism is on a downward trend, tariffs and surcharges are used in certain circumstances to protect local industries. There are also a number of other costs that are not normally incurred in domestic buying, such as international taxes, payment costs (letters of credit fees, exchange rate differentials and translation costs), commissions to customs brokers, inspection costs and customs documentation fees. Transportation costs and the additional costs to buy and hold additional inventory to avoid stockouts will be higher for international shipments. Additionally, the higher cost of expedited delivery may be necessary at times to maintain production schedules or support service delivery. The risk of obsolescence, spoilage or theft is greater as more forms of transportation are used and because delivery times usually are longer (Stanley and Matthews 2014).

J) **Environmental** — In recent years, environmental concerns have been legislated into controls and standards for industrial and consumer environmental emissions, and into disposal of industrial and household wastes — particularly hazardous wastes. Some groups believe that economic growth is to blame for increasing amounts of emissions and wastes, and that economic growth should be limited or stopped. Others believe that, for economic well being, growth must continue and that controls and incentives should be used to control the generation of emissions and wastes as well as to ensure safe disposal of those that are generated. Thus far, growth has proceeded with controls, although there are continuing debates over what amounts of emissions and wastes are safe, and debates over safe means of disposal. Other environmental concerns include land use, particularly of wetlands, and control of commercial operations on public lands, such as national forests. Laws, regulations and other decisions made to address environmental matters can affect productivity, the availability of natural and other resources, and the cost to produce products.

2) Market analysis

A) **Porter's Five Forces** — Porter's Five Forces was created by Michael E. Porter in 1980 to describe competition. The five forces are:

- The extent and intensity of direct competition

- The threat of entrants

- The threat of substitute products and services

- The power of buyers

- The power of suppliers (ISM *Glossary* 2014).

B) **Strengths, weaknesses, opportunities and threats (SWOT) analysis** — A form of risk assessment, a strengths, weaknesses, opportunities and threats (SWOT) analysis is a macro-level evaluation of an organization's internal and external forces (its strengths, weaknesses, opportunities and threats) to help senior management evaluate the organization's current environment that triggers the need for a new organizational direction, strategy or project (Stanley and Matthews 2014).

C) **Establish benchmarks through industry database** — A benchmark is a standard or point of reference used in measuring or judging an organization's performance, according to selected criteria (ISM *Glossary* 2014). An organization may choose to evaluate itself against the marketplace by accessing industry-collected benchmarks. For example, CAPS Research prepares supply management-specific benchmarks for a variety of industries.

D) **Request for Information (RFI)** — An RFI, or Request for Information, is generally used before a specific requisition of an item is issued. Most organizations will issue an RFI if they have determined there are several potential suppliers. The RFI is a solicitation document that is used to obtain general information about products, services or suppliers. It is an information request, not binding on either the supplier or the purchaser, and is often used prior to a request for bids (ISM *Glossary* 2014). The information gathered from an RFI can be disseminated throughout the organization or to specific departments.

An RFI is generally used when a large or complicated purchase is being considered and the potential pool of suppliers must be pre-qualified. In this case an RFI is a questionnaire or inquiry into the suppliers' backgrounds. It is used to determine if the supplier meets the minimum standards needed to successfully bid on the project and, if awarded, successfully complete the project.

E) **Supplier research** — Suppliers can be a valuable source regarding market conditions and trends. They may be willing to disclose new developments in their processes, products and technologies. One of the responsibilities of supply management is to gather information from suppliers.

3) Supply market complexity versus impact on business

A) **Opportunity assessment** — Each supply market will vary in its complexity. Supply management professionals should evaluate each market in terms of the degree of 1) competition, 2) geographical dispersion and 3) cooperation from suppliers. As a result, opportunities for collaboration and pricing concessions should be evident.

B) **Prioritization** — Purchased items or services will vary in their impact on the business. Peter Kraljic developed a two-by-two portfolio matrix to help supply management professionals develop an appropriate sourcing strategy for items or services purchased, based on profit impact (low to high) and supply risk (low to high). Items are categorized as strategic, routine, bottleneck and leverage.

   1.0 **Strategic** — Strategic components have a high risk-of-supply and high importance-to-competitiveness items. There are only a few suppliers, or perhaps only one, that have the technical capability and capacity to meet the buying organization's needs, so it would be difficult to switch suppliers. Expenditures for strategic items are generally high, and require supply strategies that reduce costs and ensure continuity of supply. These items are generally managed through closer win-win partnership-type relationships.

   2.0 **Routine** — These items have little effect on the organization's competitiveness and profitability. They can be easily standardized, are highly substitutable, and thus are purchased using simple contracts or procurement cards (p-cards). The ISM *Glossary* (2014) defines p-cards as a payment method whereby requisitioners are empowered to deal directly with suppliers for low-dollar, high-frequency, typically MRO-type purchases using a credit card issued by a bank or major credit card provider. The cards reduce paperwork and enable purchasing and accounts payable personnel to focus on more value-added activities. The primary goal is to minimize the procurement costs of these items while meeting immediate needs of internal customers.

   3.0 **Bottleneck** — Bottleneck items are low-value, high-risk products with customized specifications and technologies. Items in this category are generally purchased in larger quantities. Inventory levels are monitored more closely to avoid interruptions to supply. The relationship with the supplier is important to the buying organization but supply management professionals will search for alternative suppliers to avoid the risk of supply interruptions (Stanley and Matthews 2014).

4.0 **Leverage** — Leveraged items are those that have a large number of suppliers that are all capable of supplying the same product, and the dollars spent are significant (Stanley and Matthews 2014). These items are relatively low risk to obtain, yet have a major effect on the organization's competitiveness. The dominant strategy is to leverage the organization's volume to get lower prices.

4) Analytical/financial skills

An analysis of the marketplace will require a high level of analytical and financial skills. Understanding and applying price indices, economic indicators and forecasting models are just a few of the knowledge areas needed. Using these skills can minimize risks, maximize opportunities and/or evaluate innovation technologies. See Tasks in 1-B-1and Task 2-A-2 for more information.

BIBLIOGRAPHY

Cavinato, J.L., A.E. Flynn, M.L. Harding, C.S. Lallatin, M.L. Peck, H.M. Pohlig, S.R. Sturzl and V. Tucker (Eds.). ISM *Glossary of Key Supply Management Terms*, 6th edition, Institute for Supply Management®, Tempe, AZ, 2014.

Roach, S. S. "The Lessons of 2006," *Morgan Stanley's Global Economic Forum*, January 3, 2007. Downloaded January 4, 2007 from http://www.morganstanley.com/views/gef/.

Stanley, L. and D. Matthews. *Effective Supply Management Performance*, ISM *Professional Series*, Institute for Supply Management®, Tempe, AZ, 2014.

World Trade Organization (2012). International Trade Statistics 2012. Accessed June 15, 2013; https://www.wto.org/english/res_e/statis_e/its2012_e/its12_toc_e.htm

Develop supply forecasts in light of economic, competitive, technology, market and currency trends and conditions that affect procurement.

The purpose of forecasting is to develop supply forecasts in light of economic, competitive, technology, market and currency trends and conditions that affect supply management.

1) Types of forecasting

A) **Quantity** — Businesses need to predict sales quantities for new and existing products and services so they can develop demand forecasts. While estimating expected sales dollars is common practice, demand must be predicted in terms of quantity and is needed for operational planning purposes. For example, organizations need to estimate material, labor, transportation, distribution and space requirements for the upcoming year (Stanley and Matthews 2014). Price, availability, and the cyclical and seasonal characteristics are also considered when forecasting quantities of goods and services. The quantity demanded depends on the product's stage in its life cycle, as well as technological changes expected in the product and the process.

B) **Industry capacity and availability** — An organization must determine whether there will be enough industry capacity to meet overall customer demand and whether it will have the capacity to meet its share of the market. To create a capacity forecast, an organization evaluates the competition in terms of overlapping product lines and market coverage, and the expected effect on the marketplace (Stanley and Matthews 2014). If there is a need to expand capacity with an international supplier, the supply management professional should be aware of the source of the increased capacity.

C) **Cost or price** — Supply management is often responsible for performing price forecasting. Price forecasting is most commonly used for commodities such as crude oil, metals and other raw materials (Stanley and Matthews 2014). Situations for which this type of forecasting is important arise when the industries of the organization and its suppliers and customers are changing rapidly. When inputs to a finished product or service experience rapid change in price or availability, the costs to an organization and the prices charged to customers can be strongly affected. Prices can be affected by seasonality in demand patterns and by international conditions. Because of the volatility in many commodity markets, accurate forecasting of potential costs or the setting of a sale price can be complex and challenging.

D) **Technology** — Forecasting technology trends is typically done in an environment of uncertainty. Organizations need to forecast technology trends which can impact demand as products and services evolve. Technological advances can cut product life-cycle times. If an organization is not ready for those changes, a competitor most likely will be. Senior executives have to be aware of any technology gaps that may exist within their own organization and the potential threats to revenue or market share if their competitors adopt this technology.

E) **Planning** — The procurement history and economic reviews of key spending categories should represent a rigorous and comprehensive analysis of key commodity categories, including a historical review of purchases, an analysis of the present competitive environment, and forecasts of supply, demand and prices. All of these reviews should be the cornerstone of the planning activities for the supply management department and can also be used as a basic resource for other corporate planning activities. It is important to recognize that forecasting without the proper planning, research and integration of data will result in the organization being less effective than desired or required.

F) **Assuring supply** — Supply management has the responsibility to assure that supply can meet demand. In organizations that have made just in time (JIT) supply arrangements, or when supply bases are reduced to one or a few suppliers for each significant product or service, such assurance becomes critical. Forecasting supply conditions in critical markets is important to the ability to continuously ensure supply of needed items.

2) Economic concepts and terms used in forecasting

A) **Price indices** — Price indices are found by a comparison of prices in one year to a base year. A price index is a ratio expressing the relationship between the price of a commodity at a given point in time to its price during a specified base period. This information can be used to chart price level changes (ISM *Glossary* 2014). (Indices for other countries can be found at the U.S. Census Bureau web site, http://www.census.gov/aboutus/stat_int.html.)

While there are many significant economic indices, those for producer prices, consumer prices and the Gross Domestic Product (known as GDP) or implicit price deflator are among the best known in the United States. Most developed countries compute indices using economic data. There are many sources for worldwide economic data including The World Bank, the United Nations and economic research institutions at colleges and universities.

Custom indexing is a professional tool that organizations use to measure, investigate and control price and cost changes within their own organization. Custom indices are especially useful for commodities that represent a large percentage of total purchases. Supply management professionals may create a supplier price index and use it to compare against the producer price index to determine if the supplier is asking for equitable price increases. The supply management professional should be sure to identify any assumptions used to create the index.

1.0 **Producer Price Index or PPI** — The Producer Price Index (PPI) is a family of indices published by many national agencies, including the United States Bureau of Labor Statistics (BLS). Price indices of other countries are available through their respective governmental agencies. The PPI, according to the BLS, measures the average change over time in the prices received by domestic producers of goods and services. Note that the PPI is based on the selling price rather than on the actual cost to produce an item. The PPI for commodities may also be adjusted for seasonality, weather, regular marketing and production cycles, model changes, seasonal discounts and holidays when there is some economic rationale for doing so and when statistical tests indicate there is an effect present. These seasonally adjusted indices are used to analyze general price trends in the economy.

For manufacturing, these indices cover the different stages of production — raw materials, work-in-process and finished goods. Over 10,000 PPIs for individual and groups of products in approximately 650 industries are published each month and they are the first measures of inflation released each month. A list of industries not included can be found at the Department of Labor's website (http://www.bls.gov/ppi/ppinoncoverage. htm). In 2011 the department introduced an Experimental Aggregation system. According to the department's website, "This Experimental Aggregation system takes advantage of PPI's expansion of coverage over the last twenty years to include portions of the services and construction sectors by combining indexes for those sectors with the currently highlighted goods sector indexes. This new system is a model that greatly expands PPI coverage of the United States economy."

Supply management professionals and their suppliers may use the PPI to predict price inflation and negotiate price escalation clauses (Stanley and Matthews 2014).

2.0 **Consumer Price Index or CPI** — The Consumer Price Index, also published monthly by the U.S. Department of Labor and other national agencies, is one of the most popular measures of price inflation for retail goods and services. The CPI is linked more closely to labor rates than the PPI. The CPI measures the average change in retail prices over time for eight major groups with more than 200 categories of various goods and services. The rate of price inflation is important because it affects how much consumers must pay for goods and services, the cost of doing business and quality of life for those on fixed incomes. It helps businesses negotiate labor contracts and governments to establish fiscal policy. However, it represents consumer purchases only, and does not reflect product or service substitutions that consumers might make. The CPI is not useful in predicting swings in the economy because it is a lagging indicator (explained below in Tasks 2-A-2, 2C, 2.0).

3.0 **Implicit Price Deflator** — Implicit price deflator, also known as the GDP deflator, is an index used by the U.S. Department of Commerce. A deflator is a value that allows data to be measured over time in terms of some base period. An implicit price deflator is a broad measure of prices derived from separate estimates of real and nominal expenditures for the GDP or a subcategory of GDP. It is an index of prices for everything that a country produces, making it different from the CPI, which considers consumption only and includes prices of imports. The implicit price deflator was created by the U.S. Department of Commerce and compares the average level of prices in a given year to those of a base year. It is calculated using the following formula:

$$\text{Implicit Price Deflator} = \frac{\text{Current-Dollar GDP (Nominal)}}{\text{Real GDP}}$$

B) **Interest rates** — Interest is the term for the cost of borrowing money. An interest rate is the annual percentage of the principal the borrower must pay for the use of borrowed funds. Interest rates vary depending on repayment risk, duration of loan and inflation expectations. Interest rates affect investment and stimulate or depress growth. High interest rates inhibit borrowing and investment or trigger price inflation, which allows business to pass on the high cost of money. Well-known measures of short-, medium- and long-term interest rates include the following: U.S. Treasury three-month bills, U.S. Treasury notes and bonds with maturities between three and 10 years, high-grade municipal bonds, corporate AAA bonds, Federal Reserve discount rate, prime rate charged by commercial banks and new home mortgage rates. See the Federal Reserve Board at http://www.federalreserve.gov/econresdata/ for current data on interest rates and money supply.

C) **Economic indicators** — Understanding economic indicators helps supply management professionals identify those market forces that will affect the supply and demand for a particular commodity, product or service and leads to more effective material forecasts, supply management budgets and price negotiations. Some of these economic indicators are discussed in the following sections. No single indicator can give a true picture of the economy. Indicators can come from a number of sources. For example, The Census Bureau (www.census.gov) publishes The Durable Goods Report and The Factory Orders Report, while the Investment Company Institute (www.ici.gov) provides a measure of mutual fund flows in the United States. Websites such as Trading Economics (http://www.tradingeconomics.com) and The Conference Board (http://www.conference-board.org/data/bcicountry.cfm?cid=3) also publish multiple indicators by country so comparisons can be made

Indices are also published, which are expressed in a way that indicates price changes over time. The Bureau of Labor Statistics (www.bls.gov), for example, publishes the Consumer Price Index for services and The Conference Board (www.conference-board.org) releases the Index of Lagging Indicators. It is common for levels of government (federal, state, local, county prefecture, province, city, town and so forth) to develop their own indices for local business use.

1.0 **Leading** — A leading indicator is a measure of economic activity that changes before the business cycle does and thus indicates its future direction. For example, bond yields often indicate the direction of the stock market (ISM *Glossary* 2014). It is any statistic that precedes changes in economic growth rates and business activity. Some examples include the change in the number of building permits issued in a given period, the money supply (the amount of cash and bank deposits held by organizations and households), inventory level changes, average weekly hours of production workers, changes in stock prices and the number of unemployment insurance claims.

2.0 **Lagging** — A lagging indicator, on the other hand, is a measure of economic activity that tends to change after the state of the general economy has changed. A common example is the unemployment rate (ISM *Glossary* 2014). A lagging indicator confirms there has been a change in the economy, and tends to follow changes in the economy. In other words, if the economy is improving, the lagging indicators will confirm that phenomenon, and vice versa. Some key lagging indicators include labor costs, business spending, prime interest rates, inventory book value, and outstanding bank loans, as well as unemployment rates.

3.0 **Coincident** — A coincident indicator is a measure of economic activity that changes concurrently with a change in the business cycle (ISM *Glossary* 2014). Some examples include personal income, non-agricultural employment and industrial production.

D) **Inflation/deflation** — Inflation is an increase, and deflation is a decrease, in the economy's average level of prices. The rate of inflation is the percentage rate of increase in the average price level. High inflation signifies rapid price escalation and wage increases, while investment centers on tangible assets rather than on financial markets. As measured by the rate of change in the GDP deflator, the United States has not experienced deflation since the 1930s, but has experienced a persistent inflationary trend since the end of World War II.

E) **Capacity utilization** — Capacity utilization refers to the extent to which an organization, an industry or a nation uses its installed facilities. It compares actual output to potential output using the available installed capacity. The Capacity Utilization Index is computed each month in the U.S. by the Federal Reserve Board (FRB) in conjunction with the Industrial Production Index. The FRB calculates the proportion of plant and equipment used in the manufacturing, mining, and electric and gas utilities industries. This index represents the ratio of the Industrial Production Index to plant and equipment capacity (ISM *Glossary* 2014). These figures are seasonally adjusted. This is an inferential statistic, derived from year-end surveys made by several governmental and private organizations. See the Federal Reserve Board at http://www.federalreserve.gov/econresdata/statisticsdata.htm for current data on capacity utilization.

F) **Economic indexing** — An index is a comparison between a figure from a base period and a figure from a later period. This method summarizes and examines changes in the direction and level of economic activity. Index numbers relate such things as annual industrial production, industrial prices and consumer prices to those of base years.

An index typically starts with a base period or year defined as 100. The base year is often selected as a period when the economy is relatively stable, without high inflation, recession or high unemployment. All other comparison years or periods are represented as percentage differences from that base year or period. For example, if 1999 was the base year (100) for a particular statistic, and the 2013 index number for that activity was 130, then the economic activity in 2013 would be 30 percent greater than the base period.

The formula for calculating percentage changes between two periods is determined by the following formula:

$$\left[\frac{\text{current period value} - \text{prior period value}}{\text{prior period value}} \right] \times 100$$

For example, if 2005 had an index number of 105, then comparing 2013 to 2005, the results would be:

$$[(130-105)/105] \times 100 = 23.8$$

Therefore, 2013 is 23.8 percent higher than 2005 in terms of 1999 (base year) units.

G) **Gross Domestic Product (GDP)** — GDP is a measure of a nation's domestic output, which is the total value of all finished goods and services produced within a country within a given time period (typically one calendar year) (ISM *Glossary* 2014). It is a very general measure of economic activity. These are final goods and services, including only the value added at each process or distribution step. Consequently, they are purchases by households and governments, and not industry purchases. There are various components within GDP measuring activities (no in-process goods) that seek to adjust for depreciation, taxes and savings rates. Forecasting becomes more complex as organizations struggle to understand the nature of the economies of all of the countries in which they conduct business.

H) **Gross National Product (GNP)** — GNP is a measure of a nation's total output, which is the total value of all finished goods and services produced anywhere in the world by its agencies and organizations during a certain time period (typically one calendar year) (ISM *Glossary* 2014). Note that the difference between GDP and GNP is the scope of production. GDP includes only domestic output while GNP encompasses output anywhere in the world by citizens of one nation.

I) **Balance of merchandise trade** — The Merchandise Trade Balance is a measure of "visible" trade, which is trade in goods such as cars and electronics. A positive value indicates a trade surplus (exports exceed imports). A negative value indicates a trade deficit (imports exceed exports). The phrase "balance of trade" refers to the difference between the value of a country's exports and the value of its imports. The balance for a given country is favorable if more merchandise is exported than imported.

J) **Balance of payments** — The balance of payments for a given country is a measure for the difference in the flows of funds across a nation's boundaries (ISM *Glossary* 2014). It is a summary statement of a country's transactions with the rest of the world during a year. It consists of the balance of trade plus the capital account, which measures the inflow and outflow of investments and loans, and the official reserve accounts that document the changes in government reserve accounts. The United States has been in an unfavorable trade and payments position for more than fifty years.

K) **Exchange rates** — A buying organization will owe another organization based in another country a function of the international exchange rates that exist at time of payment. Historically, exchange rates had been determined under the gold standard. Each national currency was converted into a specified amount of gold. When the gold standard was abandoned, the trading nations adopted a system of fixed exchange rates. Today, international exchange rates "float" between parameters established by the central banks. Exchange rates respond to the market and to economic activity. While each country wants its currency to be "strong" relative to that of its trading partners, it does not want it to be too strong or its goods and services will be unattractive to countries whose currency is weaker. For example, a U.S. dollar that is too strong makes it more difficult to sell U.S. products abroad, because it takes more international currency to pay for U.S. products. In addition, a too-strong U.S. dollar reduces domestic investment because the dollar goes further in international investment. Differential exchange rates are exchange rates imposed by a country's government that differ, depending upon the nature of the goods or services imported (ISM *Glossary* 2014). The ISM *Glossary* (2014) defines a fixed exchange rate as a currency exchange rate set and maintained by a government. Additionally, a floating exchange rate is a currency exchange rate determined by market forces rather than government decisions.

3) Sources of data used in forecasting

The generation of fact-based or quantitative forecasts begins with research and the accumulation of data. Many sources provide useful information, including governmental data and forecasts, private organization or public organization forecasts, commercial forecasts (made available to subscribers) and internal organization data and forecasts.

A) **ISM** *Report On Business*® — Manufacturing and Non-Manufacturing — The ISM Manufacturing and Non-Manufacturing *Report On Business*® comprise two surveys of approximately 350 organizations in 18 manufacturing industries and 18 non-manufacturing industries from around the country. Unlike other business system indicators, the ISM *Report On Business*® does not measure the level of activity, but the month-over-month change in activity level. Supply management professionals from these organizations are asked to report changes from the previous month for several activities. The main indicators for which change is reported are production, new orders, supplier performance, inventories, employment and commodity prices. Supply management professionals report whether each activity was higher/better than, the same as, or less/worse than the previous month. For each of these indicators, a "diffusion index" is formed by adding all the "higher/better" responses with half of the "same" responses, to develop the indicator. Five of the manufacturing indexes — at equal weights — are included in the ISM PMI™ composite index. A reading over 50 indicates the manufacturing economy is generally expanding; a reading below 50 indicates the manufacturing economy is generally contracting. Changes in the PMI™ index historically have had a close relationship to changes in GDP. Because the first government estimate of GDP for a quarter is not available until one month after the end of the quarter, the first month's PMI™ for the quarter gives an early indication of that quarter's GDP three months before the first government number is available.

A composite index for the non-manufacturing sector, the NMI™, was first released in early 2008, and is comprised of four of the non-manufacturing indexes with equal weights.

The ISM *Report On Business*® is among the most widely watched and highly regarded of all leading economic indicators. The report has two specific advantages. First, turns in diffusion (change) indices have the property of leading turns in the actual activities, when changes are measured by one quarter of a business cycle. Second, unlike governmental data, which are often several months old when released, the ISM data describe changes in the previous month's activity. For these reasons, the ISM *Report On Business*® is extremely valuable as a macroeconomic forecasting tool. More information on the manufacturing and non-manufacturing *Report On Business*® can be found at www.ism.ws.

B) **Government publications (international and U.S. domestic)** — Federal, state and local governmental agencies gather and publish a remarkable variety of information on a broad range of business and economic topics. In most metropolitan areas in the United States, there are libraries designated as federal depositories that contain information disseminated by the federal government. A document librarian is essential when researching government documents. Many universities, including those internationally, are part of consortiums that share government publications from around the world can be accessed by anyone. The U.S. Government Printing Office (GPO) is a source for many popular federal publications. The GPO website, http://www.gpo.gov/fdsys/, provides access to a wealth of electronic documents and links to other federal agency websites. Most countries have a wide array of national and international economic data available; however, the explanation of the data may be in the native language. Most embassies and consulates have sources of information since their mission is to enhance trade activities. In addition, several additional organizations including the United Nations, World Trade Organization, International Monetary Fund and The World Bank could be useful in obtaining economic data. The U.S. Department of Commerce and state commerce departments offer many types of statistical information useful to forecasters.

C) **Private publications** — Many associations, such as the Institute for Supply Management (ISM) and various industry associations, publish surveys or analyses of economic conditions for their members. Special interest groups also generate information that would be useful. Other business forecasts can be found in *The Wall Street Journal, Business Week* or the *Financial Times*.

D) **Commercially prepared information** — Many organizations develop and market economic forecasts for sale to subscribers. Among these are banks and industry groups. Customized forecasts are available from many of these organizations.

E) **Regional surveys** — Many of the local affiliates of ISM publish their own business surveys. These surveys, which are similar in methodology to the ISM *Report On Business*® , reflect local or regional situations that may be significantly different from national conditions.

An up-to-date listing of the regional ISM surveys is available at www.ism.ws. Each state in the United States also has economic data. The Europa World Yearbook and its website are sources for economic data for a variety of countries.

F) **Internal historical data** — Many organizations develop organization-specific forecasts from their own internal historical data. For example, forecasts of sales for individual products and families of products can be determined using internal records. Forecasts of standard costs, lead times, seasonality of demand, employment levels and financial data are additional types of internal historical information that can be gathered and used.

G) **Industry sources** — Industry publications, newsletters and associations specialize in particular industries.

H) **Online indices and search engines** — Most economic data can be found on the Internet at various industry, association and government websites. Much of this is available free of charge, but some require a subscription or membership, or are offered as reports that can be ordered. The Internet is an excellent source of international data that may be needed for forecasting supply and demand in countries around the globe, and understanding international conditions in the marketplace. International statistics are often segmented by developed nations, developing nations or newly industrialized countries, emerging markets and developing countries. Countries within a given classification are more likely to operate similarly and different from countries in another classification due to variations in income levels and capital available for international exchange. Three international organizations that provide extensive statistical data include the United Nations (UN) at http://www.un.org/, the Organization for Economic Co-Operation and Development (OECD) at http://www.oecd.org, and the International Monetary Fund (IMF) at http://www.imf.org/. The United Nations provides international trade statistics and a world economic survey, among other publications. UN COMTRADE, for example, is a report on global commodity trade statistics that is available online.

4) Forecasting methodologies/techniques

In any comprehensive forecasting program, many methods of forecasting are applied. The technique chosen varies based on the type of forecast, the data available and relevant to the forecast, the time frame in which the forecast is needed, and the technology and budget available for the forecasting process. Several of the most important characteristics and methods related to forecasting are discussed below:

A) **Short-term versus long-term**— Long-term and short-term forecasts are often made. A short-term (usually up to one year) forecast is used as an aid in the development and execution of short-term purchase plans and operational or tactical activity. Long-term forecasts facilitate the evolution and development of strategic plans and typically include in-depth commodity and industry studies.

B) **Macro versus micro** — Macro forecasts project broad scale activities, such as a nation's gross national product or an industrial sector such as the services sector or farm sector.

Micro forecasts are organization specific, or limited to small segments of larger issues. Macro and micro forecasts usually are linked. An organization may forecast prices paid for a specific, locally purchased product (micro), but that forecast will be dependent on the status of that supply industry nationally and globally (macro). An organization's projection for the next year's inventory investment is based on sales estimates which, in turn, are based on general economic condition forecasts.

C) **Delphi method** — Many times, supply management professionals need forecasts of activities or issues for which no factual data exist. A procedure for developing such opinion-based forecasts is the Delphi method. First used by the Rand Corporation in 1963, this procedure begins with the identification of a panel of experts in the field of interest. Rather than bring these people together, they are deliberately kept apart and are unknown to each other. This is done because group dynamics and discussion may distort and reduce creativity. These experts are posed a series of questions regarding the topic. Each expert then prepares a written response to each question, along with supporting arguments. Each participant receives anonymous copies of all other responses. The experts are then invited to revise or defend their responses. Next, the revisions are submitted to the researcher, who repeats the process perhaps as many as three or four times, until a consensus develops. Uses for the Delphi method may include sales revenues, including long-range forecasting for product and service demand, developing projections for new product demand and predicting technological developments. The Delphi method can be used to forecast societal changes, scientific advances, the competitive environment or government regulation and may be useful in directing an organization's research and development. The results from use of the Delphi method can be used with other analytical tools to create a most-likely scenario forecast.

D) **Correlation/regression analysis** — Correlation analysis and linear regression analysis are methods for measuring the statistical, but not causal, relationship between two variables. Measures of correlation are used to describe the degree of relationship between two data series (ISM *Glossary* 2014). The correlation coefficient indicates whether the linear relationship is positive (both increase together) or negative (one increases while the other decreases). With the use of a regression equation, the value of one variable based on the other variable can be predicted. Correlation and regression analyses are particularly useful for forecasting estimates when historical data exist and there is reason to believe the current relationship between variables will continue.

E) **Time series** — Time-series analysis is a method for examining the factors that influence changes in data series over time. These factors include trends, cyclical variations, seasonal fluctuations and random influences (ISM *Glossary* 2014). The underlying assumption is that a forecast can be created based on patterns observed within the time-series data. Time-series analysis for costs, prices, inventories, interest rates and employment is important to business because it can be used to extract information regarding variations that might be time-related. To accurately forecast based on time-series data, reasons for variation must be examined. To use time-series analysis to the best advantage, it must first be determined whether fluctuations in the observed data stem from seasonal variation, long-term general business or economic variation due to business cycles, long-term trends, or are merely the result of random sampling error. Sometimes all of these factors are causing variation in the data, and must be teased out of the data using statistical techniques. Data may be smoothed and seasonally adjusted to remove these influences, with the objective of exposing the long-term underlying relationship.

F) **Central tendency** — In any data set, the statistics of interest may lie in the measures of central tendency, because these statistics allow generalized interpretation. Measures of central tendency include the mean, mode and median. The mean is the average of all of the values in the set. The mode is the most frequently appearing value in the set. The median is the midpoint when the set is arranged from lowest to highest value.

G) **Variability** — Central tendency shows only part of the picture. Measures of variability or dispersion, the degree to which values of the variables of interest differ from each other, are important. The smaller the measure of variability, the more tightly the numbers cluster around the central point. Measures of variability include range, variance and standard deviation. The range of a set of numbers is the largest number minus the smallest. The variance equals the squared sum of the differences of the individual values of a set from the mean, divided by the number of values in the set. The standard deviation is the square root of the variance. Both the measures of central tendency and the measures of variability are useful to describe a data set and the relationships within a set of values for one variable. These measures may be used to determine other statistics when a set of data contains values for more than one variable. One such statistic is the correlation coefficient between two variables, which is determined using correlation analysis described briefly in section D, above.

H) **Analysis of cyclical data** — A cyclical component of data is the residual variation fluctuating around the long-term trend, due to changes in the economic or business system. A cycle is longer than a season, often a multiyear phenomenon, and is tied to economic fluctuations such as recessions or inflation. A cycle is among the most difficult patterns to predict. Economic indicators and indices are generally used to predict cycles. Seasonality is the name given to a pattern that is observed regularly, occurs for a constant length of time, and is influenced by given seasonal factors such as day of the week or a given monthly quarter. Seasonality can be applied to hour-of-the-day variations, in which there are certain times of day that are always busier than others and can be used to forecast resources needed to handle peak demands in service industries. The existence of seasonality is usually easy to observe if there are enough data points to plot the data. For monthly data, a plot of two years of data (24 data points) will usually reveal seasonal patterns, if they exist. More data is better and can be used to confirm patterns. Since cycles can be much longer, sometimes as much as 50 years, it is a rare circumstance to have enough data to identify cycles by plotting the data.

Economic cycles and seasonal patterns can often make detection of long-term trends difficult. For this reason, data are often seasonally adjusted, meaning that the cyclical or seasonal component of the data is removed and the data is smoothed. The objective is to uncover the long-range, underlying trend in the data to see if there is a sustainable increase or decrease in demand. (Trends are discussed in the following section, I, below.)

Smoothing is a process that dampens variations in data to make trends more apparent. A moving average is applied to two or more periods of data, and a new set of data is created. For seasonal variations that appear to be quarterly, one may apply a three-month moving average to the data to smooth it. A statistical technique called exponential smoothing weights the observations being averaged to give more weight to the most recent data.

I) **Trend analysis (future sales based on past sales)** — An increasing or decreasing pattern of demand over time is considered a trend. A trend is the long-term component that underlies change in a series of data. Some of the factors that produce trends include population changes, productivity changes, technology changes, supply/demand changes and price changes. Trends may be discerned by plotting smoothed data. The trend can be described statistically using exponential smoothing, regression analysis or other appropriate techniques. When trend and seasonality are present, the use of Winter's Model (otherwise known as triple exponential smoothing) or seasonal exponential smoothing is commonly applied. Reliable software is available to estimate trends using the Winter's Model.

J) **Decision tree analysis** — The decision tree is one means to help supply professionals make interdependent decisions under uncertain conditions. A decision tree is a decision-making tool that maps alternative courses of action and their consequences. Its components include decision forks, outcome forks, outcome probabilities, outcome rewards and expected values (ISM *Glossary* 2014). Decision trees are useful because they give some structure to decision-making and provide a more objective way of analyzing the alternatives. Computer software packages are available which make the process relatively easy.

K) **Box-Jenkins** — The Box-Jenkins Method is similar to linear regression; however, it is more complex. This method can be used when the data in a time series are stationary (when the mean remains constant and there are no trends) or can be transformed into a stationary series. The first step is to use a statistical method to determine if the model is autoregressive (when past demand is a good predictor of future demand), a weighted moving average (in this case, the weights do not add up to 1 and the weights are usually higher for more recent values), or both. The forecaster estimates the model using regression. Then, some diagnostic checking is performed to assure a correct fit of the model. Computer software is available to make the process easier.

L) **Exponential smoothing** — The advantage of exponential smoothing is that relatively little data is required. The Delphi Method is used first to estimate the initial forecast. Then, demand for the most recent period and the estimated forecast for the previous period are used to calculate the current forecast using a weighting method.

5) Factors that can affect forecasts

The numerical output of any forecasting tool is accurate only as long as conditions remain unchanged. Factors that can affect the accuracy of forecasts include war and threats of war, strikes and threats of strikes, and natural factors such as disasters, discoveries and depletions. Other issues for consideration include changes in technology, government, law and the population, or consumer tastes. Each of these and other commodity-specific factors must be considered and tracked for each of an organization's critical raw materials or components.

A) **Fluctuating lead times** — Fluctuation in lead times may result in material shortages or require larger inventories to protect the organization from delivery uncertainty. Both of these situations increase costs, so neither is acceptable in today's globally competitive economy. Factors causing lead time fluctuation range from financial and production problems, to demand increases, to constrictions in a supply chain. Many of these can be measured and forecasted. In planning material acquisitions, the supply management professional must carefully assess the probability of occurrence and causes of lead time fluctuations and work with suppliers to decrease or eliminate those fluctuations where possible.

B) **Changing labor conditions** — Any organization that purchases materials or services from organizations or supply chains that contain organized labor needs to be aware of upcoming labor agreement expirations and the accompanying potential for supply disruption. Not only can labor negotiations affect a supplier, they may disturb output from an entire industry. Strikes, or threats of strikes, can result in dramatic market changes. Advance warning of such potential supply constrictions allows a supply professional to take protective action. Additionally, labor issues in countries or regions where the organization has suppliers must be carefully monitored.

A surplus or shortage of specific labor skills may also inhibit or enhance the ability of an organization to supply its customers. For example, a lack of skilled machinists or electronic technicians may restrict output of products requiring those skills. Availability of specific requisite labor skills should be observed and forecast in the same way as availability of other necessary inputs.

Strikes, threats of strike and shortages of properly trained skilled labor are elements of potential change to historical projections that the supply management professional must track and forecast for all critical purchased materials and components.

C) **Changes in money markets** — Early theories of international trade assumed that a country's factors of production (land, labor and capital) were fixed and immobile. In today's economy, funds are transferred worldwide around the clock. Money markets in financial centers all over the world facilitate currency exchange and lending. Central banks operate in concert to regulate exchange rate limits and interest rate differences. Because many businesses have suppliers and customers around the globe, tracking these fluctuations may become the purview of the supply management professional.

In the United States, the Federal Reserve Board (the U.S. central bank) has the delicate job of balancing the availability of money in the national economy. Making funds more readily available has the benefit of driving interest rates down, but risks growth in the rate of inflation. Restricting money supply counteracts inflation, but results in higher interest rates that limit or restrict business expansion and affect unemployment.

At the micro or organizational level, an increase in interest rates obviously affects an organization's borrowing rate and its cost of doing business. It may cause a project to be "crowded out" — to become economically unattractive to the organization. In an economic sense, reductions in investment lead to reductions in income and employment.

D) **Geopolitical factors** — A geopolitical environment is defined by the political situation of a region given its geography, history, religion, government structure and socioeconomic factors. As companies continue to expand into global markets, geopolitical risks have increasingly affected them. Some common risks include terrorism, war and political corruption.

Changes in government often portend changes in the business climate. Even in the United States' relatively stable political system, a change in the political party in power may bring about change in emphasis on anti-trust law enforcement, environmental focus, economic goals regarding money supply, inflation and acceptable levels of unemployment. In other countries, political change, or even the threat of political change, may pose significant risk to a multinational organization and outsourced supply. Supplies or prices of raw materials or components purchased from politically unstable countries may change precipitously. As a result, supply management professionals need to have a comprehensive contingency plan to cope with unexpected events and ensure supply continuity.

E) **Technological shifts** — In our current environment of rapidly changing and developing technology, shifts from an established technology to a new one can significantly affect forecasts. For example, the rapid development and adoption of the Internet as a means of locating sources, communicating with suppliers and conducting business transactions caught many businesses unprepared in the late 1990s and early 2000s. That shift in technology came so rapidly that many established organizations paid little attention to it at first, giving new organizations opportunities to enter the market and take market share. Those organizations that have lost market share as a result were well aware of the impact of technological shifts on forecasts. While such shifts are difficult to foresee, and their impact even more difficult to predict, forecasters must be vigilant for continuing rapid technological developments and include these possibilities in forecasts as alternate scenarios, whenever appropriate.

F) **Climatic conditions** — In the longer term, weather can play a critical role when considering the amount of sunlight and moisture necessary for materials originating with agricultural products. In the shorter term, it can adversely affect the ability to extract minerals and transport goods. At its extreme, weather can idle suppliers' plants due to flooding or wind damage, as well as interrupting their supply of power, water and gas utilities. In recent years there have been examples of extreme disasters such as tsunamis, floods, earthquakes and hurricanes that have shut down entire regions of the world. The potential for supply disruption can be mitigated to some extent by disaster planning on the part of supply management professionals.

G) **Changes in global trade** — Shifts can affect the relative supply and demand for goods and services, but the sources precipitating these shifts are also of importance. Changes in customs duties, trade embargoes and import quotas can change availability, but political instability may limit supply, especially when civil unrest occurs. Supply management professionals also need to be aware of government subsidies that artificially lower the price of goods and the impact of developing nations acquiring higher levels of technological capability.

H) **Changes in economic conditions** — Shifts in the economy affect forecasts. Some specific indicators that could be considered include consumer spending, business investments, level of inflation, unemployment rates and trends in new construction. It is important to consider a wide array of economic indicators to obtain a true picture of local and global economies and their respective impact on supply and demand.

I) **Data integrity** — It is critical that data being used for forecasting is accurate and current. Managers pull data existing in enterprisewide systems, including past purchasing, sales and usage information, as well as data from many external sources. The most accurate forecasts that senior management can rely on can only be created from accurate data.

6) Measures of forecast accuracy

No forecast will be 100 percent accurate. It is up to the forecaster to measure how well the forecast performed against actual demand. Three measures commonly used are described in the following sections:

A) **Standard error** — When a population is normally distributed, standard error of the mean is the population standard deviation divided by the square root of sample size (ISM *Glossary* 2014).

B) **Mean squared error** — In statistics, the mean squared error (MSE) is a measure of the total error to be expected for a sample estimate. The forecast is subtracted from the actual demand for each time period for a given sample of data, to determine the error. Squaring the errors removes the chance of working with negative numbers (ISM *Glossary* 2014).

C) **Mean absolute percent error** — Another measure of forecast error, the mean absolute percentage error (MAPE), is calculated by dividing the absolute forecast error by the actual demand for each time period, summing the percentages, and then dividing the total by the number of time periods included in the analysis. This method gives the forecaster a good idea of the true magnitude of forecast error because, similar to the mean squared error (MSE), absolute values are used in the formula.

BIBLIOGRAPHY

Cavinato, J.L., A.E. Flynn, M.L. Harding, C.S. Lallatin, M.L. Peck, H.M. Pohlig, S.R. Sturzl and V. Tucker (Eds.). ISM *Glossary of Key Supply Management Terms*, 6th edition, Institute for Supply Management®, Tempe, AZ, 2014.

Czinkota, M. R., I. A. Ronkainen and M. H. Moffett. *International Business*, 7th edition, John Wiley & Sons, 2011.

Patton, M. G. *Purchasing Economics Forecasting — Planning to Stay on Top*, *presentation* at ISM's 92nd Annual International Supply Management Conference, May 2007.

Stanley, L. and D. Matthews. *Effective Supply Management Performance*, ISM Professional Series, Institute for Supply Management®, Tempe, AZ, 2014.

United States Bureau of Labor Statistics, http://www.census.gov/#.

Yuva, J. "The Global Reality of Global Politics," *Inside Supply Management*®, November 2009, p. 18.

Task 2-A-3
Manage forecasted data with suppliers.

1) Business forecasting models

Business cycle forecasting models rely on leading indicators, which measure economic activity that changes before the business cycle changes and thus indicates its future direction. Some examples include the change in the number of building permits issued in a given period, the money supply (the amount of cash and bank deposits held by organizations and households), inventory level changes, changes in stock prices, the number of unemployment insurance claims, average hours worked per week and new orders.

2) Confidentiality issues

The basis for early supplier involvement is trust between the parties. Part of this trust is built on the confidentiality of the information shared between the organizations. Confidential information may take a variety of forms, such as bids, supplier proposals, pricing, drawings, designs, strategies, wage and salary information, software programs or scientific formulas. The supply management professional should ensure that information about one supplier is never given to another supplier unless laws and regulations require that the information be made public — as in the case of public procurement.

The other internal participants in the procurement process may not be aware of the need for confidentiality. Therefore, it is supply management's responsibility to ensure that proper controls are established to protect information. One way to protect confidential information is to put it in writing and label all affected documentation "Confidential." Another tool is the nondisclosure agreement (NDA) that clearly defines acceptable and unacceptable uses of the information.

3) Parameters for disclosure

When an organization and a supplier are developing a new product or service, it is important to create an agreement in advance that specifies when and under what conditions the information developed (bids, supplier proposals, pricing, drawings, designs, strategies, software programs or scientific formulas) may be released to others.

A) **Product development model** — Many organizations are concerned with protecting their intellectual property. The safest way to avoid problems is to not allow access to trade secrets or other proprietary information. Intellectual property agreements can take many forms, ranging from complete ownership by the supply management organization to complete ownership by the supplier.

B) **Production plan** — It is common for organizations to share production plans with suppliers. The supplier should regard the production plan as confidential. It is appropriate to use a confidentiality or nondisclosure agreement that includes a section describing the supply management professional's commitment to the schedule. For example, an organization commits to 100 percent of the first four weeks of the schedule, plus or minus 10 percent for the second four weeks, and plus or minus 25 percent for the third four-week period.

4) Legal implications

When using nondisclosure agreements, "proprietary information" must be carefully defined. If it is too broad, the supplier or supply management professional may not want to sign the agreement, and it may be difficult to enforce. If it is too narrow, the supply management professional or supplier risks exposing and losing important data. Try to be specific. Consider software, customer lists, pricing information, target markets, business plans and other material not usually shared with competitors. The definition usually will state that publicly available or generic information is not proprietary. The supply management professional might want to include a dispute resolution clause, in the event problems arise about what data is proprietary.

The NDA should define how information may be used. How many copies of the documents can be made? Who gets to see and use the proprietary information? The contract should require the return of the data if the venture is not successful or the relationship ends.

A well-drafted, mutual NDA should prevent each party from disclosing the other party's confidential information to third parties. It should limit the use of the other party's confidential information to the authorized purposes that are set forth in the NDA. This latter provision is designed to ensure that neither party's confidential information will be used in a manner that was not anticipated by such party. An NDA will often provide that the recipient will treat the confidential information with the same level of care that they use to protect their own confidential information. This language can be dangerous because the recipient may not be taking adequate steps to protect their own information. The agreement should obligate the recipient to use at least reasonable care to protect the other party's confidential information.

5) Supplier-managed inventory (SMI)/Vendor-managed inventory (VMI)

Supplier-managed inventory is an inventory management system that holds a supplier responsible for ensuring that stock is maintained at appropriate levels in the supply management professional's facility and for replenishing items when these levels drop. This is also sometimes referred to as vendor-managed inventory, or VMI (ISM *Glossary* 2014).

6) Collaborative Planning Forecasting and Replenishment (CPFR)

CPFR is an initiative developed by the Voluntary Interindustry Commerce Standards (VICS) Association that allows collaborative processes across the supply chain.

Some of the first applications of CPFR involved a final retailer sharing its consumer demand forecasts upstream in the supply chain to enable manufacturers of branded goods to produce and distribute their products to the retailer at lower costs.

CPFR originated in the United States in 1996, through an initial pilot that involved a large retailer (Wal-Mart) and one of its key suppliers (Sara Lee). After this initial pilot, VICS published a set of guidelines for organizations to follow.

The primary driver for the adoption of CPFR is the frequent misalignment in the forecasts developed by different organizations in the supply chain, leading to problems such as misallocated inventory, which leads to excess inventory (leading to excessive holding costs or mark downs) or to stockouts (leading to loss of sales).

CPFR is, in some ways, an extension of supplier managed inventory (SMI), with more collaboration between the supplier and retailer in the process of developing forecasts and managing exceptions. Figure 1 (below) provides an overview of the process.

CPFR has primarily been applied between retailers and their suppliers, though the principles can be applied by any two adjacent organizations in the supply chain. Enterprises are starting to experience the limits of accruing business benefits out of supply chain management within their own boundaries. This is leading enterprises to extend their supply chains beyond their own boundaries to involve business and trading partners.

CPFR enables the joint deployment of best practices such as category management and supply chain planning and execution processes throughout the organization, including but not limited to the sales and supply management organizations.

CPFR has the capability to minimize stockouts, which reduces supply chain costs while improving overall customer service.

Figure 1

Retail Event Collaboration Process Overview
(VICS CPFR Model)

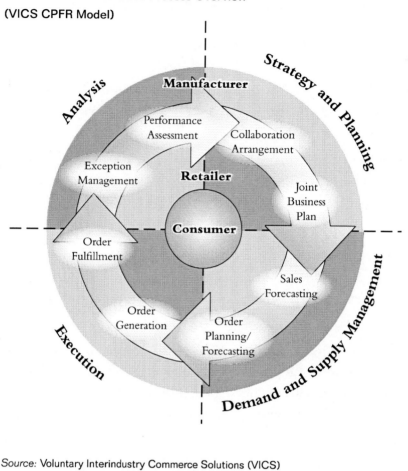

Source: Voluntary Interindustry Commerce Solutions (VICS)
Association Retail Event Collaboration Process Overview,
VICS CPFR®, Model 2004.
CPFR is a Registered Trademark of VICS.

7) Product life cycle

There are a number of ways suppliers can be actively involved during each stage of the life cycle of a product. The product life cycle consists of five stages or phases: pre-commercialization, introduction, growth, maturity and decline. During pre-commercialization, suppliers may contribute by developing component specifications; by recommending parts, new technologies or processes; or by co-developing products.

In the introduction phase, suppliers can proactively monitor quality and correct problems before they reach the customer organization, adjust production and delivery schedules based on actual demand and collaborate with supply management to make changes as necessary.

During the growth phase, supply management may share forecast data with its suppliers to ensure continuity of supply. In the maturity phase, suppliers might manage inventory (supplier managed inventory) and in the decline stage the suppliers may offer lower-cost solutions or parts to substitute for the initial product.

Throughout the product life cycle, sustainability is increasingly an ongoing concern. Throughout the life cycle, procurement must ensure there are processes in place for making sourcing decisions that have a positive effect on sustainability. Procurement begins by developing a set of sustainability initiatives and then sourcing from sustainable suppliers. It is also important to encourage suppliers to set their own sustainability goals, and track their results. During the relationship, procurement conducts supplier sustainability reviews to ensure each supplier is in compliance and implements improvement programs if necessary. As part of each review, procurement collects and analyzes supplier data in order to manage its own sustainability initiatives.

8) Information exchange options

Information shared between the supplier, supply organization and all parties involved may be exchanged using a number of formats including: face-to-face meetings, virtual meetings, conference calls, email, Web portals or other systems integrations using various technologies.

BIBLIOGRAPHY

Adapted from the C.P.M. Study Guide, 7th edition, Institute for Supply Management®, Tempe, AZ, 2001.

Cavinato, J.L., A.E. Flynn, M.L. Harding, C.S. Lallatin, M.L. Peck, H.M. Pohlig, S.R. Sturzl and V. Tucker (Eds.). ISM *Glossary of Key Supply Management Terms*, 6th edition, Institute for Supply Management®, Tempe, AZ, 2014.

Stanley, L. and D. Matthews. *Effective Supply Management Performance*, ISM Professional Series, Institute for Supply Management®, Tempe, AZ, 2014.

Voluntary Interindustry Commerce Solutions (VICS) Association Retail Event Collaboration Process Overview, VICS CPFR®, http://www.vics.org/docs/committees/cpfr/CPFR_Overview_US-A4.pdf. Model 2004, CPFR is a Registered Trademark of VICS.

Logistics

Task 2-B-1

Design/modify logistics facility layouts and equipment designs to support business model, increase productivity and lower operating costs.

The logistics process affects nearly all dimensions of human interaction, yet we often do not consider the role of logistics in our daily interactions until something goes wrong. Supply management professionals recognize the impact of the logistics of moving and storing their goods, including in the areas of cost, flexibility, time and delivery performance. Advancing technologies have found application in the management of logistical operations and, together with the realities of globalization, are creating challenges and new opportunities that were nonexistent a few years ago. In short, logistics has evolved into a strategic imperative for many supply management professionals because of the profound impact on performance and the investments made to link to the organization's customers. The ISM *Glossary* (2014) defines logistics as the process of planning, implementing and controlling the efficient, cost-effective flow and storage of raw materials, in-process inventory, finished goods and related information from point of origin to point of consumption for the purpose of conforming to customer requirements.

1) Considerations for geographical location

A) **Labor**— An important component of any logistics organization is labor because workers will ultimately determine an organization's success. It is therefore vital that employees' skills and abilities, pay scales, training programs, selection and retention procedures and other employee-related issues be considered in selecting and locating the logistics organization.

B) **Transportation availability** — Selecting transportation carriers is important in making the facility location decision because their availability, adequacy and cost will affect the proximity of plants, warehouses and retail locations to the final consumers.

C) **Governmental issues** — The location of production plants, warehouses, offices and retail locations are governed by federal laws, state statutes and local zoning ordinances. Every country, state and local government has different zoning ordinances. The organization must ensure that their buildings meet those requirements.

    1.0 **Political** — To bring in new industry, some countries, state and local governments are willing to offer tax breaks and other financial concessions to bring new jobs into their area. For example, Brazil in 2013 instituted specific tax incentives to aid the struggling ethanol industry (http://www.platts.com/RSS-FeedDetailedNews/RSSFeed/Oil/21976172). Local officials may be eager to attract new industry, particularly with a declining economy. However, other areas may not be inclined to do so, as they represent constituents that do not wish to see their community grow or may not want industry in their neighborhood (Stanley and Matthews 2014).

2.0 **Tax considerations** — In most U.S. states, an organization is at a definite advantage if it owns no property there, because such ownership means the organization is doing business in the state and is therefore subject to various, and potentially substantial, state taxes. Therefore, it may be advantageous to use for-hire carriers and public warehousing. Many U.S. states do not assess taxes on inventory in public warehouses, creating an additional tax shelter for in-transit and stored inventories. Other countries, such as India, use tax incentives regarding warehousing to entice organizations to build in their country.

D) **Environmental considerations** — Keeping the environment clean and healthy for the future has become an important responsibility for the supply professional. The challenges of effectively managing an organization without harming the environment can be successfully surmounted if the right tools and practices are available. State and federal oversight agencies such as the Department of Transportation, Environmental Protection Agency, and Occupational Safety and Health Administration (OSHA) all regulate matters concerning hazardous materials/waste, recycling, clean air and compliance auditing. A source for international environmental information is the Center for International Environmental Law (CIEL). There are numerous local, regional and national environmental organizations that supply management professionals should know about if they are doing business in a particular country.

E) **Channel proximity/modality**— The purpose of the channel is to provide consumers with the goods they desire, in the right combinations at minimum cost. Consumers determine channel location and structure with purchase patterns that drive the logistical service output requirements. The best channel is said to be formed when no other competing entity generates higher profits and consumer satisfaction per dollar of cost. Given a desired level of output by the consumer and competitive conditions, supply chain intermediaries will arrange their processes and functions in a way that minimizes total costs. This shifting of specific processes leads to the entry and exit of service providers in the channel.

F) **Average delivery time** — Average lead time is one indicator of logistics performance. However, in many business situations, management must be able to deal with variability in lead time. Transportation delays along with supplier and production problems make lead time variability a fact of doing business. Also, remote or global logistics facilities will increase both average delivery time and the variability in delivery time.

2) Considerations for layout

A) **Build out versus build up** — Organizations must make the decision whether to expand a facility vertically, otherwise known as build up, or horizontally, referred to as build out. The height of the building will dictate how high shelving can be assembled, which is a key consideration in warehouse design. The higher the shelf racking, the better the space utilization. Therefore, in addition to square footage or meters, it is important to consider cubic footage or meters. Vertical capacity requirements relate directly to the type of equipment that will be needed. See Task 2-B-1-2-F. for more information on warehouse equipment (Stanley and Matthews 2014).

B) **Two dock versus single-dock layout** — Loading dock design has entered a new era of sophistication, thanks to practices such as just in time inventory. Such practices require docks to accept more frequent deliveries from trucks of varying sizes. Management has traded off 90-day stocks for two-hour supply limits. Therefore, today's loading docks must be more flexible and efficient than ever before. A sound understanding of material handling, inventory control, safety requirements and legal statutes is required. Good dock design contributes to logistics, safety, efficiency and profitability of the business operation. Guidelines for accomplishing this include:

- Position the building on the site and the doors on the building to allow safe access to roads and the dock area.

- Arrange the loading dock to accommodate trucks of all sizes. The dimensions of the dock door, the dock height, and the location of the landing strip all factor into this decision.

- Assist those responsible for material flow to get through the docks. They are best able to judge dock equipment on the basis of safety, productivity, reliability, capacity and flexibility.

- Plan the staging area inside the loading dock so material flows efficiently to and from its internal destination.

C) **Safety** — The one area where carriers and their customers cannot compromise cost is safety. The added pressure of moving high volumes of freight more efficiently often requires compromises in the length of time between repairs and replacement of operational equipment. Supply management professionals need to be cognizant that if a carrier develops a reputation for unsafe operations, such as having too many accidents, a loss of customers will likely ensue.

D) **Security** — The level of required security is a key issue with managing facilities (plants, warehouses, etc.), particularly with the increase in terrorism. If the entire facility is secure, then the need for guards and gates is limited. Controlling ingress and egress, keeping parking areas away from the immediate vicinity of the building and designing the building to be difficult to penetrate limit the cost of securing the facility. Alarm systems are useful deterrents, but not impenetrable. In most facilities, losses come from internal theft. Therefore, control of ingress and egress should be coupled with a verifiable document system to limit this risk.

E) **Sanitation** — Waste disposal is another consideration. Transportation and manpower costs will vary depending on the distance to the local landfill. Supply management professionals must consider local and governmental regulations regarding substances that may be banned from dumping, such as certain chemicals, and any recycling requirements. The availability of sewage systems must also be a factor.

F) **Warehouse material handling systems (for example, facility forklifts, pickers, etc.)**

Forklifts — The forklift has enabled significant productivity growth for the receiving, storing, picking, staging and loading functions of the warehouse. In fact, most products spend more time in the material handling process than in the manufacturing process. Forklifts chosen for an application must be integrated into the product flow within the warehouse or manufacturing facility.

Pallets — The most common method of supporting a unit load is with the use of a pallet. Pallets have provided a useful service since forklifts were developed, and allow for ease and efficient movement of unit loads by forklifts. They are produced in various materials, sizes and designs. The most common materials include wood, corrugated paper, plastic, steel and aluminum. Wooden pallets are available in most geographic locations and can be easily repaired. Plastic pallets are being used because they can be reused almost indefinitely. Corrugated pallets can be erected as needed, thus reducing space requirements.

Pallets provide a useful function but are an added cost to a material handling system. Supply management professionals must adequately design the return process, which adds complexity to operating processes and a consideration in locating logistics facilities.

Warehouse receiving — Receiving entails scheduling appointments with carriers for specific unloading times. Most carriers appreciate a scheduled receiving dock and are most cooperative with organizations that use appointment systems because the systems represent obligations. Running a scheduled receiving operation requires the ability to measure and predict work flows to allow the warehouse to hold to scheduling timetables. The increasing use of advance shipping notices (ASNs), an electronic manifest, facilitates the receiving process more efficiently and accurately. An ASN is defined in the ISM *Glossary* (2014) as a notification in electronic data interchange (EDI) or extensible markup language (XML) format, sent ahead of a shipment, listing its contents and shipping information. It often includes purchase order numbers, stockkeeping unit (SKU) numbers, lot numbers, quantity, pallet or container number and carton number. It is usually combined with bar-coded compliance labeling for easy scanning, receipt into inventory and automated data collection. ASNs may also be paper-based.

G) **Labor intensive versus mechanized** —Materials handling is most typically a labor-intensive process because it is done either manually or semi-manually. The goal is to find the best warehouse layout, equipment and degree of automation that will optimize materials handling and thus minimize costs.

A) **Automation** — The ISM *Glossary* (2014) states an automated warehouse is a storage facility that uses one or more automation technologies, such as automated storage/retrieval systems (AS/RS), automated guided vehicle systems (AGVS) and/or radio frequency identification systems (RFID). Automation includes automated palletizers, and hand-held bar code readers. AS/RS equipment enables highly accurate, real-time management of inventories because of its capacity to keep precise records of all item counts by location in storage while ensuring security of materials. Because of their ability to densely pack inventories in often unused overhead space, AS/RS frees up large amounts of floor space, permitting major expansions in production volume without the need for additional new space. The process of RFID is increasingly used to positively impact the management of inventory. RFID is a passive or active radio data chip that is attached to products to allow retailers to track access and compile data as part of the supply-chain flow process (ISM *Glossary* 2014).

B) **Picker-to-part versus part-to-picker** — The most traditional material handling approaches to order picking require the picker to travel to the storage location. Without a stock location system, this involves searching as well as traveling. However, traveling is a non-value-added activity and should be minimized. The types of picker-to-part methods include pick-to-pallet, pick-to-cart, pick-to-roller and man-aboard storage/retrieval. Part-to-picker systems include carousels, storage conveyors and AS/RS.

3) Order picking versus stock replenishing functions

Order picking involves the outbound flow of materials from an organization's warehouse to its customers while stock replenishment is the inbound flow of materials from suppliers to the warehouse.

Orders must be prepared, or picked and packed for delivery to a staging area. Thus, reducing order picking time should be considered in the design of the materials handling system. Items on a picking-route list should be arranged so an efficient route is created through the stock found in the warehouse to reduce handling. Backtracking in aisles and past the same stock should be avoided to minimize time and cost. Software programs are used to sequence orders into efficient pick lists.

Stock replenishing is key to ensuring that the organization maintains the optimal level of stock that is cost effective and minimizes the on-hand inventory. One replenishment method is based on independent or random demand. It is usually end-customer driven and has a high level of uncertainty. Independent demand uses a reorder point/level system for inventory management. A reorder point system is a continuous review inventory control system in which an order is placed whenever a withdrawal brings the inventory position to a predetermined reorder point level (ISM *Glossary* 2014). Another replenishment method is the dependent or predictive demand method. Dependent demand is derived from or contingent upon the demand for another component or a finished product. It is driven by the demand of the supplier or customer order. It enables more anticipation and certainty than the independent or random demand. Dependent demand uses resource planning systems such as MRP or MRPII.

4) Virtual warehouse versus physical warehouse

Traditionally, organizations operated with bricks-and-mortar warehouses. All inventory would travel through the organization-owned warehouse before being shipped to an internal or external customer. With a virtual warehouse, actual buildings and real inventory still exist, but inventory for sale may not be stored in an organization's warehouse. Instead, inventory is shipped directly from the supplier's warehouse. If an item is not in stock, an organization might authorize it to be shipped directly from the supplier to the customer. This is possible due to the advent of real-time information sharing through the integration of information systems between organizations. The advantages of virtual warehousing are that an organization can offer a wider variety of products to its customers without stocking them, potentially generating more revenue; also, the cost of maintaining large and/or multiple warehouses is reduced.

5) Logistics performance measures, strategies and cost-savings initiatives

A) **Cost-to-sales ratios** — These ratios are used to evaluate organizational effectiveness. As with any measure used in practice, there are issues related to which costs, logistical functions, overhead (managerial salaries, for example) and sales (net versus gross) should be included in the metric.

B) **Logistics cost per unit versus budget** — Controlling costs through predetermined standards (a benchmark) and flexible budgets is regarded as the most comprehensive type of control system available. Standard costs reflect what the costs should be if the organization is operating efficiently. Supply management professionals then devote decision-making to variances from the budget. The use of standard costs represents a direct approach to determining and assigning logistics costs. However, the use of standards may not be appropriate in scenarios involving the performance of nonrepetitive tasks, and for which work-unit measurements are difficult to establish. Four basic types of budgets are used in logistics financial controllership: fixed dollar (static), flexible, zero level and capital. In practice, most logistics budgets remain static rather than flexible. A fixed-dollar (static) budget is an estimate of functional expenses. A flexible budget accounts for seasonal and internal factors that drive activity costs beyond budgeted levels. Zero-level budgeting assigns all costs necessary to perform a range of support services for functional units and funding is developed in a zero-up manner, in which funds are justified on the basis of planned activity. Capital budgeting specifies the amount and timing of significant financial investments for logistics resources.

C) **Cost of functions as a percent of sales** — A productivity ratio, the cost of a function (such as logistics) compares the annual amount spent on logistics resources (workers, operational activities and overhead) to sales revenue. Although sales will vary from year to year, the ratio should remain the same or change in an expected way.

D) **Inventory turns (for example, sales/inventory, cost of goods sold [COGS]/inventory)** — In many organizations, management attempts to improve profitability by emphasizing the need to improve inventory turnover. Emphasis on inventory turns requires that decision-makers also consider the needed process improvements and breakthrough improvements (such as collaborative forecasting and planning). Pushing for increased inventory turnover without consideration of the impact on total logistics costs may lead to decreased profitability.

E) **On-time delivery** — Organizations depend on timely delivery of goods to support their operations. Late deliveries are troublesome because scheduled work activities can be delayed until the order is received unless safety stock is available. Early deliveries, in contrast, can create other problems. For example, if a delivery arrives earlier than expected, additional holding costs are incurred as the order is waiting to be processed. Organizations may use an ABC system to categorize purchases ("A" items are the most important items strategic to the business). They expect "A" items to be on-time, while allowing more leeway for "B" and "C" items. On-time delivery is typically measured as a percentage of on-time deliveries divided by all deliveries.

F) **Scorecards** — A scorecard is a performance measurement and management document that records the ratings from a performance evaluation process (ISM *Glossary* 2014). For an organization to improve its logistical performance using the scorecard method, it must begin by defining its vision and goals. Then, it should determine the logistics strategies that will lead to attaining its vision and goals. These strategies should be operationalized into specific performance-driven activities. Performance measures can then be developed for each activity. For example, inbound activities might be measured by dock utilization, pallet putaways, number of case receipts per man-hour and receipt volume (backlog).

6) Third-party and fourth-party logistics considerations (3PL and 4PL)

Third-party logistics services may be provided by a party other than the manufacturer or seller, or the party buying or receiving. The third party, not directly involved in the transaction, provides one or multiple services such as warehousing or transportation. Thus, the third party should be considered in the design or modification of an organization's logistics system as if activities were being performed in-house. The trend in warehousing is to move toward the increasing use of third-party logistics and warehousing providers. The service provided by the third-party provider is their core activity. The client organization is then able to release many fixed costs and decrease headcount (Cavinato, Flynn and Kauffman 2006).

Fourth-party logistics providers (4PLs) are entities established to provide the management of both inbound and outbound materials, parts, supplies and finished goods for other organizations. A 4PL is often a separate entity established as a joint venture or long-term contract between a primary client and one or more partners that act as a single interface between the client and multiple logistics service providers. Ideally, all aspects of the client's supply chain are managed by the 4PL (ISM *Glossary* 2014).

7) Process improvement action plans

Troublesome performance (for example, costs are rising or productivity has declined) will require finding ways to improve or change the current logistics process. To take corrective action, the underperforming process should be reviewed, underlying factors determined and an action plan developed to make improvements. Process improvements should not occur only when there are issues. Continuous process improvements should be addressed throughout the life of the partnership. Process improvements are a joint interaction and involvement among all parties.

Another process improvement method that offers a practical approach to improvements, whether at the office, logistics function or the warehouse, is the 5S discipline. By assigning everything a location, time is not wasted looking for items. It is quickly obvious when something is missing from its designated location. 5S advocates believe the benefits of this method come from deciding what should be kept, where it should be kept and how it should be stored. It is a concept that originated in Japan. The five levels are listed below.

- Sort (Seiri) — Keep only essential items that can be stored efficiently. This makes the workplace free of clutter, which encourages productive work.

- Set in order or arrange (Seiton) — Focus on the concept of an orderly workplace and items are kept where they will be used.

- Shine (Seiso) — Keep the workplace clean and neat.

- Standardize (Seiketsu) — Standardize work practices so that individuals know what their responsibilities are.

- Sustain (Shitsuke) — Continuously improve and train.

BIBLIOGRAPHY

Ballou, R.H. *Business Logistics*, 5th edition, Pearson Education Inc., Upper Saddle River, NJ, 2004.

Cavinato, J.L., A.E. Flynn and R.G. Kauffman (Eds.). *The Supply Management Handbook*, "*The Physical Supply Chain Design and Linkages*," p. 240, 7th edition, McGraw-Hill, New York, 2006.

Cavinato, J.L., A.E. Flynn, M.L. Harding, C.S. Lallatin, M.L. Peck, H.M. Pohlig, S.R. Sturzl and V. Tucker (Eds.). ISM *Glossary of Key Supply Management Terms*, 6th edition, Institute for Supply Management®, Tempe, AZ, 2014.

DePaoli, Thomas M. "Measuring Effectiveness," *Purchasing Today*, November 1996, p. 4.

Emmett, S. *Excellence in Warehouse Management*, John Wiley & Sons, Hoboken, NJ, 2005.

Environmental Protection Agency. www.epa.gov, October 2007.

International Tax Review, www.internationaltaxreview.com, September 2007.

Stanley, L. and D. Matthews. Effective Supply Management Performance, ISM *Professional Series*, Institute for Supply Management®, Tempe, AZ, 2014.

Task 2-B-2

Direct traffic/distribution policies and procedures to ensure optimum flow of material and consolidation of freight.

1) **Transportation modalities** — In a 2012 survey conducted by ISM, 79 percent of the respondents indicated that transportation, traffic management and shipping were either part of their job responsibilities or supervisory responsibilities, or the responsibility of someone in the supply management organization. The decisions made by an organization regarding transportation are important in today's world. The decisions are vital as supply chains become longer, more complex and increasingly external. A long-term focus, collaboration with transportation providers and technology are the keys to successfully moving freight in the supply chain. According to a 2013 study by the National Shippers Strategic Transportation Council (NASSTRAC — a shipper's association), companies are developing long-term transportation strategies that tie to their supply chain strategies. Shippers are also teaming with transportation providers to improve productivity by optimizing their computer networks, changing modes as necessary, investing in new and enhanced technologies, and cutting transit times. Transportation rates, reliable on-time delivery and financial stability are the most important criteria in carrier selection and companies regularly benchmark rates and services (NASSTRAC 2013).

There are five modes of transportation: water, motor carrier, rail, air and pipeline. Each has unique characteristics. (See Task 2-B-3, 1 for more detail on the characteristics.) When considering a transportation modality, the supply management professional should assess the following factors:

- Types of goods to be transported, including size, weight, density, packaging and specific physical characteristics

- Which mode or combination of modes will be best suited to meet the organization's needs

- Delivery requirements, including the time needed.

- Organizational requirements.

Third-party and fourth-party logistics providers are frequently used with international sourcing. As discussed in Task 2-B-1-6, these services provide many benefits.

2) **Transportation restrictions** — There are multiple rules and restrictions concerning transportation. For example, all carriers have weight and volume restrictions. There are laws restricting the transportation and handling of hazardous materials. There are policies regarding border crossing inspections and security measures.

3) **Carrier cost auditing** — To control transportation costs, organizations will typically implement audit procedures to review freight bills. Human error calculating rate variances, descriptions, weights and routing are all possible, resulting in overcharges. Organizations often outsource this activity to a third party known as a freight bureau (Stanley and Matthews 2014).

4) **Carrier performance auditing** — Carrier performance must be optimal to ensure value to the customer. Some areas of performance that should be monitored and reviewed include willingness to work as a partner, commitment to continuous improvement, acceptance of innovation, focus on time reduction, flexibility in logistics systems design and commonality of core values (Stanley and Matthews 2014).

5) **Freight classifications/rates** — Line-haul rates are charged for the movement of goods between two points that are not in the same local pick up and delivery area. Due to deregulation, most rates today are negotiated and set into contract form between shippers, receivers and carriers. Their economic basis stems from former regulatory standards such as class and distance. The class system categorized goods according to value, density and susceptibility to damage and theft. Today, a carrier evaluates a new shipper's goods according to these factors and then applies a distance cost rate to them. In many cases, this is just a starting point, because shippers/receivers can negotiate better rates, typically through discounting, by using such things as total volume with the carrier, favorable directional or seasonal flows, better packaging, faster loading and unloading, and other economic and business factors.

6) **Available technology** — Electronic commerce and the use of information technology is common in logistics, especially in the area of traffic management. Computerized transportation activities can be categorized into four groups: transportation analysis, traffic routing and scheduling, freight-rate maintenance and auditing, and vehicle maintenance.

   - Transportation analysis — This software allows supply management professionals to monitor costs and service by providing historical reporting of key performance dimensions.

   - Traffic routing and scheduling — This software provides features such as the sequencing and timing of vehicle stops, route determinations, shipping paperwork preparation and vehicle availability.

   - Freight-rate maintenance and auditing — This software maintains databases of freight rates that are used to rate shipments or to perform freight bill auditing.

- Vehicle maintenance — Features that are commonly provided by this type of software include vehicle maintenance tracking, scheduling and reporting.

7) **Relocation or movement processes** — When considering the relocation or movement of products, supply management professionals should consider any physical restrictions, such as warehousing, methods of transportation and amount of material needing to be relocated or moved.

BIBLIOGRAPHY

Ballou, R. H. *Business Logistics*, 5th edition, Pearson Education Inc., Upper Saddle River, NJ, 2004

Cavinato, J.L., A.E. Flynn and R.G. Kauffman (Eds.). *The Supply Management Handbook*, 7th edition, McGraw-Hill, New York, 2006.

NASSTRAC. "Freight Transportation 2013: The State of the Industry Report," http://www.nasstrac.org/, accessed June 2013.

Pinkerton, R. and E. Marien. "Fourteen Steps to an Effective Transportation Program," (2:8), *NAPM InfoEdge*, April 1997.

Stanley, L. and D. Matthews. *Effective Supply Management Performance*, ISM Professional Series, Institute for Supply Management®, Tempe, AZ, 2014.

Manage international transportation, invoicing and documentation functions to ensure corporate compliance with all governmental import, export, hazardous material and air freight regulations.

1) Modes of transportation and impacts

There are five basic modes of transportation: motor carriage, rail, air, water and pipeline. Each mode has its own unique advantages and disadvantages. Motor carriage, commonly known as trucking or highway transportation, is highly competitive with a few large and many small carriers. The majority of shipments are semifinished or finished goods. Few goods are moved without highway transportation at some point.

Trucks are frequently used for shipments across borders in the European Union and within the United States. Trucking organizations also are often hired to complete ocean shipments. Truck organizations fall into two categories:

- Less-than-truckload (LTL), which collect smaller shipments and consolidate them into full truckloads; there are a few large LTL carriers

- Truckload (TL), which is made up of many small carriers that own one or two trucks.

Rail accounts for approximately 40 percent of all freight movements, carrying primarily low-value bulk cargo (for example, food and wood products) and raw materials (for example, coal and lumber), but containers and trailers also are now commonly moved on freight cars. Railroads also offer other special services, such as guaranteed expedited service or stop-offs to load or unload. Rail service is often available at ocean ports to continue the movement of international shipments to their destination.

Air transportation is a major component of an organization's logistics program due to the increase in global manufacturing. There are constraints when using this mode, including physical characteristics of the product such as dimensions of the shipment. Shipments commonly include replacement parts, small high-value items and mail.

Water shipping provides service where rail or truck is not feasible. It is a low-cost option for transporting large quantities of product globally or over inland waterways. However, at least one other mode, such as air, rail, or truck, is generally needed to complete the freight movement to its final destination. Thus, organizations must determine the most effective combination of modes to ensure efficient freight movements. Water transportation helps promote international trade. Demand for container ships is on the rise, and there can be issues with port congestion.

Lastly, pipelines are a special category of transportation, limited to the movement of crude oil, refined oil products and coal slurry.

A) **Cost/mode trade-offs** — Air transportation is the most expensive, followed by trucking, rail, pipeline and water. The decision on which combination of modes to use and when will be heavily influenced by the needs of the organization and its customers. Each mode of transportation should be considered based on four areas: transit time, predictability, cost and non-economic factors. Considerations regarding transit time would include the length of time available for product delivery, whether it is an emergency situation or if the product is perishable. Ocean and air freight are subject to natural occurrences that would make them less predictable. However, air transport delays tend to be shorter in duration. Tracking is another aspect of predictability that should be considered. For multinational organizations, the ability to track products for multiple locations is an important consideration. Because air freight is the most expensive, this cost must be justified based on market demand. The physical density, value of the cargo and the supply chain considerations of the organization will contribute to this decision. A non-economic factor contributing to the decision is governmental influences. Some governments may require organizations to use national carriers (Czinkota, Ronkainen and Moffett 2011).

B) **Multimodal shipments** — Multimodal shipments, also known as intermodal shipments, are those involving more than one mode of transportation, for example, rail and motor, motor and air, rail and water, and air and truck.

Ideally there is a seamless transfer of goods between each mode, facilitated by information flows. The supply management professional should be aware that each transportation mode exerts a different set of stresses and strains on the products being transported. The development of intermodal containers that fit on trucks, ships, railroad cars and airplanes can ease the transfer of goods and provide better use of carrier space. The containers also provide some protection from pilferage and damage. However, when transporting domestically or internationally, the proper handling facilities must be available for transfers. Otherwise, the products would need to be unpacked then reloaded, thus increasing the costs of the shipment (Czinkota, Ronkainen and Moffett 2011).

2) Roles of shipping companies, customers, suppliers and freight forwarders

- Shippers — The originator (sender) of a shipment, typically the seller or supplier

- Customers — The acquirer/recipient of an organization's outputs

- Suppliers — An organization that provides goods and/or services to a supply management organization

- Freight forwarders — A third-party service provider that makes transportation arrangements and fills out forms under power of attorney. Freight forwarders combine small shipments from multiple shippers into full loads. Because full loads are less costly, they receive a price discount from the carrier. They make a profit on the difference between what they charge the shipper and the discounted price.

3) Import/export documentation

There are multiple documents that may be required to import or export goods as shown in the following table:

Export document	Description
Bill of lading	Cargo receipt and transportation contract between shipper and carrier. Equivalent documents are the air waybill, sea waybill and multimodal bill of lading.
Transmittal letter	Record of all documents that will accompany the shipment and their final disposition, along with any special instructions.
Letter of credit	Document that assures the seller that payment will be made by the bank issuing the letter of credit upon fulfillment of the terms of the sales agreement.
Certificate of origin	A statement of precisely where (in what country) the goods were produced.
Commercial invoice	Bill for the goods to the buyer.
Dock receipt	Transfers the responsibility for the cargo between the international and domestic carrier.
Delivery instructions	Directives to an inland carrier for delivery.
Insurance certificate	Proof of insurance for goods while in transit.
Export declaration	Required government form to track exports for statistical purposes.
Consular invoice	A control document to track and identify goods shipped to other countries.

Import document	Description
Arrival notice	Declares a shipment's expected arrival time and relevant shipment details.
Delivery order	Authority from the consignee to the ocean carrier to release the cargo to a specified inland carrier.
Customs entries	Multiple documents that describe the shipped merchandise, origin of shipment and applicable duties.
Freight release	Statement that all freight charges have been paid.
Carrier's certificate and release order	Certification of ownership of the cargo provided to customs.
Special customs invoice	Official government form used to declare the value of the shipment.

4) Traffic patterns

Congested airways, highways and waterways are always a factor in estimating delivery lead times. Carriers commonly use on-board navigation systems to provide real-time information about current traffic conditions, warnings about traffic congestion and accidents. These systems are often used in conjunction with routing and scheduling software to enable the immediate rerouting of vehicles and rescheduling of upcoming deliveries.

5) Shipping routes

Considering the significant capital investment in equipment and facilities, good routing and scheduling is central to achieving acceptable levels of profit and customer service. Yet routing and scheduling are very complex processes because there may be many vehicles, customers and routing combinations to consider. Good routing and scheduling can reduce transportation costs and increase productivity. The use of prescheduled shipments, the management of pickup and delivery frequencies, the use of fixed routes instead of variable route, and working with delivery time windows represent practices leading to measurable gains from managing shipping routes. There are a number of routing and scheduling software packages available, which can aid the process.

6) Incoterms® rules

The Incoterms® rules are a set of standard delivery terms developed by the International Chamber of Commerce (ICC), primarily for use in international shipping. There have been several versions of these terms. The ICC has approved a new version of the terms, designated Incoterms® 2010 rules, which became effective January 1, 2011.

For some time the Incoterms® rules have consisted of 13 terms. Incoterms® 2010 rules eliminates four of the previously existing terms (DDU, DES, DEQ and DAF) and adds two new terms (DAT and DAP), resulting in a total of 11 terms. The new version is made available for both domestic and international use; contracting parties should, however, review the applicability of these terms to the domestic environment prior to applying them.

The terms have been structured to increase incrementally the obligations (control, risk and cost) on one party while decreasing the obligations of the other, depending on the specific term chosen. Each term clarifies which party is responsible for:

- Inland freight (transportation within the origination country)

- Forwarder selection

- Export clearance

- Carrier selection and scheduling

- International freight

- Import clearance

- On-carriage (transportation within the destination country).

Delivery occurs (and risk of loss transfers) at the point designated by the term selected. Transfer of title is not covered by any of the Incoterms® rules and must be separately specified by the parties.

The Incoterms® rules can be divided into two groups — multimodal (available for multiple forms of transport, including land, air and waterway transportation) and single mode (applicable only to waterway transportation).

The multimodal terms are:

- Ex works (EXW) named place (seller's premises)

- Free Carrier At (FCA) point in seller's country

- Carriage Paid (CPT) point in buyer's country

- Carriage Insurance Paid (CIP) point in buyer's country

- Delivered Duty Unpaid (DDU) point in buyer's country — this term is eliminated in Incoterms® 2010 rules

- Delivered at Terminal (DAT) port, airport, terminal — this term is added in Incoterms® 2010 rules

- Delivered at Place (DAP) point in buyer's country — this term is added in Incoterms® 2010 rules

- Delivered Duty Paid (DDP) point in buyer's country.

The single mode terms (which can only be used with waterway transportation) are:

- Free Alongside Ship (FAS) vessel

- Free On Board (FOB) vessel

- Carriage & Freight (CFR) ocean or river port

- Carriage Insurance Paid (CIP) point in buyer's country

- Carriage, Insurance & Freight (CIF) ocean or river port

- Delivered Ex Ship (DES) ocean or river port — this term is eliminated in Incoterms® 2010 rules

- Delivered Ex Quay (DEQ) ocean or river port — this term is eliminated in Incoterms® 2010 rules

- Delivered at Frontier (DAF) — this term is eliminated in Incoterms® 2010 rules.

The terms in each group are listed above in order of increasing responsibility for the seller (and correspondingly, decreasing responsibility for the buyer). For example, using the term EXW makes the seller responsible only for making the goods available at its own premises; delivery occurs and risk of loss transfers at that point. When the term DDP is used, the seller becomes responsible for everything except on-carriage where the location for delivery is not the buyer's actual location. DDP is the only Incoterm® rules that makes the seller responsible for import clearance.

Buyers in the United States who are likely to be familiar with delivery terms defined within the Article 2 and 2A of the Uniform Commercial Code (UCC) should pay particular attention to the overlap in the use of certain terms/abbreviations between the Incoterms® rules and the UCC. Free on board (FOB), free alongside (FAS) and carriage, insurance and freight (CIF) are all used in the UCC, but their definitions there are much different from the definition of the same terms in the Incoterms® rules. Under the Incoterms® rules, all three of the overlapping terms (FOB, FAS and CIF) fall into the "single mode" group, meaning they can only be used for waterway transportation. Under the UCC, only FAS is limited to use with a vessel.

Note: Although the new Incoterms® 2010 rules became available for use as of January 1, 2011, Incoterms® 2000 rules (the previous version) will continue to be available. It is incumbent upon contracting parties to determine which term they want to use and to designate the version being applied.

Numerous publications and seminars are available through the International Chamber of Commerce (http://store.iccbooksusa.net/) as well as from other organizations explaining in depth the application of both Incoterms® 2000 rules and Incoterms® 2010 rules.

Incoterms® rules is a registered trademark of the International Chamber of Commerce.

7) Security considerations (for example, U.S. Customs-Trade Partnerships Against Terrorism [C-TPAT])

With the increase in global procurement, supply management professionals must assess the risks associated with, and take steps to ensure the safe delivery of, freight. This means considering potential risks (for example, terrorism, hijacking, theft, government instability), assessing where the supply chain is vulnerable, and the potential consequences from a breach in security.

Two important approaches to combating these threats are C-TPAT and ISO 28000. C-TPAT is a joint government-business initiative to build cooperative relationships that strengthen overall supply chain and border security. Through this initiative, the U.S. Customs and Border Protection Service asks that businesses ensure the integrity of their security practices and communicate their security guidelines to their business partners (importers, carriers, brokers, warehouse operators, manufacturers and so on) within the supply chain. The International Organization for Standardization has created a standard, known as ISO 28000, against which organizations may apply for independent certification of their supply chain security management system (SCSMS) (ISM *Glossary* 2014). ISO outlines the requirements for setting up, implementing, operating, monitoring, reviewing, maintaining and improving an SCSMS using a continuous improvement process. The objective is to help organizations protect cargo movements within the supply chain and facilitate global trade.

8) Hazardous and regulated materials

Supply management professionals must be concerned with the packaging and movement of hazardous and regulated materials, which include but are not limited to explosives, gases, flammable liquids and solids, poisons and corrosive metals. Supply management professionals have the greatest influence on what should be purchased because of their knowledge of the products, materials and services that are on the market. Thus, they should look for nonhazardous products as replacements for hazardous ones when possible. If a switch is not possible, it is important to comply with any laws and regulations regarding the movement and disposal of hazardous and regulated materials. Both the Environmental Protection Agency (EPA) and the European Union, for example, have strict regulations including documentation and audit requirements. To make sure hazardous materials are moved safely and comply with federal, state and local laws, supply management professionals should receive systematic and recurrent training.

BIBLIOGRAPHY

Ballou, R.H. *Business Logistics*, 5th edition, Pearson Education Inc., Upper Saddle River, NJ, 2004.

Cavinato, J.L., A.E. Flynn, M.L. Harding, C.S. Lallatin, M.L. Peck, H.M. Pohlig, S.R. Sturzl and V. Tucker (Eds.). ISM *Glossary of Key Supply Management Terms*, 6th edition, Institute for Supply Management®, Tempe, AZ, 2014.

Czinkota, M. R., I. A. Ronkainen and M. H. Moffett. *International Business*, 8th edition, John Wiley & Sons, 2011.

International Chamber of Commerce. www.iccwbo.org/products-and-services/trade-facilitation/Incoterms-2010/, June 2013.

"New Suite of ISO Supply Chain Management Standards to Reduce Risks of Terrorism, Theft, and Fraud." http://www.iso.org/iso/home/news_index/news_archive/news.htm?refid=Ref1086, Oct. 25, 2007.

Stanley, L. and D. Matthews. *Effective Supply Management Performance*, ISM *Professional Series*, Institute for Supply Management®, Tempe, AZ, 2014.

Manage the resolution of delivery/receiving problems including freight loss and damage claims.

1) Freight terms (domestic and international)

Incoterms® rules are the common standard for specifying freight terms and were described in detail in Task 2-B-3. When resolving delivery/receiving problems, the supply management professional should first refer to the Incoterm® rules used in the contract.

2) Delivery tracking systems

Real-time tracking systems are typically used by large organizations to determine shipment dates, determine where a shipment is at any given point in time and when delivery has taken place. These systems allow the shipper to take remedial action when necessary or redirect cargo to respond to a sudden need elsewhere. Technology has improved how supply management professionals can track their products, and this trend will continue. The increased usage of radio frequency identification (RFID) systems will add to the information provided in tracking systems. It will be able to provide real-time communication.

3) Delivery performance measurements

Delivery performance is an important determinant of customer satisfaction. So the primary objective is for the supplier to deliver the required materials or services on time. Some measures frequently used to measure whether a delivery is satisfactory include:

- Damages: Amount per vehicle

- Damages: Amount to goods while in transit

- Damages: Amount to goods during loading

- Damages: Amount to goods while unloading

- Late deliveries as a percent of all deliveries

- Percent of orders delivered on time

- Percent of deliveries outside preset delivery windows

- Cost of damage claims.

4) Visible versus latent damage

Damage can be visible — sometimes called unconcealed loss or damage, or latent — sometimes called concealed loss or damage. Visible damages are easy to detect during routine inspection. An automobile delivered with a cracked windshield is an example of visible damage. Latent, on the other hand, is not easy to detect. A latent defect is one that is hidden and is therefore unnoticeable during inspection. An air compressor that looked fine when delivered, but was later found to have a faulty electrical switch, would be an example of latent damage.

The buyer of the goods has protection in cases of both visible and latent damage. Goods that are visibly damaged can be refused for delivery or can be replaced at no additional cost to the buying organization. The damage should be noted on the carrier's delivery receipt to substantiate the liability. The organization should keep a copy of the receipt. Latent damages can be a bit more challenging, particularly if the defect is discovered after time has passed. A concealed loss or damage may be difficult to collect because it is difficult to determine where the damage occurred. However, the supply management professional may still invoke warranty rights to replace or repair the item (Stanley and Matthews 2014).

5) Rules for freight claims

Freight claims, as defined in the ISM *Glossary* (2014), are claims against a carrier due to loss of, or damage to, goods transported by that carrier; also for erroneous rates and weights in assessment of freight charges. The basis for filing a freight claim is a breach of contract and the claimant must initially prove its claim. Once it has been determined that the goods were undamaged at the point of shipment but arrived damaged, the burden of proof then shifts to the carrier.

The procedures and forms used are generally standardized across all modes. Claims handling involves the actual recording, handling and monitoring of product claims arising from carrier-responsible loss or damage. Accurate, real-time data collection is important. Organizations are advised to keep historical records for the purpose of identifying trends in loss and damage, and response times for claims payments. The time limit for filing a claim varies by mode of transportation. Because of the increase in international shipments using more than one mode, it also can be difficult to determine which mode was responsible for the damage.

6) Resolution processes

A typical resolution process consists of at least two key components: Escalation and corrective action.

A) **Escalation** — A shipment may be damaged, lost, incorrect or late. In these circumstances, the parties involved must settle the dispute. Initially, the supply management professional should contact the shipper or carrier to rectify the situation. If the shipper or carrier fails to rectify the situation, the supply management professional may take the next step and file a claim. To help determine whether responsibility lies with the shipper or the carrier, receiving personnel should strictly inspect incoming goods and record any issues or problems (for example, damaged boxes, short orders).

Some negotiation may be required to resolve the claim; this type of negotiation is a critical skill for supply management professionals. Narrowing the differences in a dispute can allow both parties to give a little and arrive at a mutually agreeable resolution. When both parties end a negotiation feeling content with the outcome it is a win-win proposition. However, this is not always possible; in the event a claim cannot be settled amicably, litigation may be necessary. Litigation can be costly and time consuming for all involved. Although the judicial system is available to all, it is often preferable to resolve differences outside of the courts.

B) **Corrective action** — To avoid escalation of claims and satisfy the customer, the carrier or shipper has the option to take corrective action before a claim is filed. For example, a carrier communicates to the shipper and receiver that the goods have been lost in transit. It then seeks to retrieve them. In the event the goods cannot be found, a claim is filed immediately by the receiving organization. If an over-shipment has been made, the buying organization can either keep the additional goods and pay for them, or return them to the shipper for a refund. In the case of damaged goods, the responsible party may offer to replace or repair them, or the receiving organization may do the repairs and charge the party responsible for the damage.

7) Freight audit procedures

To control transportation costs, organizations need to implement procedures for auditing their freight bills. Many mistakes in billing occur as a result of human error, which can include variances in rates, descriptions, weights, duplicate invoicing, wrong payment terms and routing. A large organization can experience between 3 percent and 5 percent overcharge in its freight bills each year. While the auditing function can be performed internally or externally, many organizations find it beneficial to outsource this service. A small organization can find it particularly advantageous to do so, as they likely do not have a staff person for this function. Organizations that perform freight auditing are called freight bureaus. They normally provide service on a percentage or commission basis (Stanley and Matthews 2014).

8) Maritime law (for example, general average)

An important principle of Maritime law is known as the General Average. In brief, should any cargo be thrown overboard or any expenses incurred because of an emergency situation while en route between ports, all losses will be split proportionally between the parties that hold a financial interest in the voyage. This principle is often referred to as the York-Antwer Rules, which provide the details for applying the General Average.

9) Reverse logistics

Supply management professionals are increasingly concerned with product returns, packaging reuse, minimization of waste and repairs that flow back into an outbound supply chain. The objectives of reverse logistics (RL) are cost reduction, environmental benefits and source reductions (ISM *Glossary* 2014). Successful reverse logistics programs can improve customer service as well as financial performance.

BIBLIOGRAPHY

Ballou, R.H. *Business Logistics*, 5th edition, Pearson Education Inc., Upper Saddle River, NJ, 2004.

Cavinato, J.L., A.E. Flynn, M.L. Harding, C.S. Lallatin, M.L. Peck, H.M. Pohlig, S.R. Sturzl and V. Tucker (Eds.). ISM *Glossary of Key Supply Management Terms*, 6th edition, Institute for Supply Management®, Tempe, AZ, 2014.

Farris M. T., II, D. Maserang, T.L. Pohlen and J. Tognazzini (Eds.). "Transportation and Related Services," *The Purchasing Handbook*, 6th edition, McGraw-Hill, New York, 1999.

Force, R., Yiannopoulos, A.N. and M. Davies. *Admiralty and Maritime Law, Vol. 2*, Beard Books, Frederick, MD, 2006.

Johnson, P.F., Leenders, M.R. and A.E. Flynn. *Purchasing and Supply Management*, 14th edition, McGraw-Hill, New York, 2010.

Primus, B.W. "Freight Claims in Plain English," *Logistics Management*, July 2012, pp. 46-48.

Stanley, L. and D. Matthews. *Effective Supply Management Performance*, ISM Professional Series, Institute for Supply Management®, Tempe, AZ, 2014.

Materials and Inventory Management

Task: 2-C-1

Develop/implement a material and/or service standardization program.

1) General issues in standardization and simplification

A) **Advantages and disadvantages** — Standardization in materials, processes and layouts can lead to efficiencies and cost savings. The objective of standardization and simplification is to reduce the complexity and number of required parts, operations, SKUs, specifications, work instructions, suppliers and processes that an organization requires to produce its products and services and conduct business with its customers. Standardization can result in reducing non-value-added activities and decrease the total cost of ownership. Some of the other advantages of standardization and simplification are increased profitability, decreased cycle time, improved quality, lower maintenance costs and more consistency. The interchangeability of specific products or services leads to broader utilization across the enterprise. Standardization may allow an organization to deal with fewer suppliers, purchase in larger quantities, lower inventory cost and reduce training costs.

There are some disadvantages to standardization and simplification. Reliance on fewer suppliers may limit competition, customer choices and opportunities for new products and services. The introduction of the standardized part or process may require a new contract and new relationship with suppliers. There may be costs of introduction, training, installation, and development of instructions, procedures and processes associated with the change to standardized parts or processes as well as testing procedures to ensure quality. Supply management professionals should strike a balance between immediate cost savings and total cost of ownership issues. Time and development costs, and any cost effects on other parts of the business should be carefully analyzed.

B) **Procedures or steps in applying**

1.0 **Committees** — When an organization embarks on a standardization program, a committee should be appointed to administer the program, develop the standards, evaluate requests for standardization and for exceptions to standardization, set policy and participate with suppliers. A standardization committee should involve a cross-functional team that includes members from supply management, engineering, sales, operations, finance and other appropriate representatives, including suppliers and customers. The objectives of the committee are simplification of design and reduction of total cost of ownership, which includes the purchase price of a good or service and additional costs incurred before or after product or service delivery.

The team should have a sponsor or a champion to manage the milestone timing and the return on investment. The committee should always keep the objectives of their task in the forefront. Spending numerous hours and funding with little or no results will not reach the objective desired. The sponsor/champion can also help facilitate decisions for which the team has reached an impasse, and will be responsible for removing any obstacles in the project reporting progress to senior management.

2.0 **Involvement of other departments** — In a manufacturing environment, engineering and supply management will likely be the drivers of the process and others will be primary stakeholders. In service environments, the project may be driven by supply management, a specific line of business or business unit, or staff support functions such as human resources or marketing. Finance will make key contributions related to costs, inventory or asset management. Some of the best ideas can come from end users working with the parts, or from members of the team not as closely vested in the product or service. All stakeholders having an interest in or are affected by standardization and simplification programs should have an opportunity to contribute to the process.

3.0 **Effects on production methods/operations** — In manufacturing, standardizing will almost always produce improvements in reducing setup time and create longer production runs, which can result in improvements in efficiency and lower operating cost per component part.

In non-manufacturing or service environments, supply management has equally beneficial reasons to implement these programs. Even without a product, significant productivity gains can be achieved in processes and procedures that could have a positive cascading effect for the business. Standardization and simplification have the capacity to reduce non-added-value activity to the overall operations.

4.0   **Effects of global operations** — It is important to take global requirements into consideration in any standardization and simplification program. In manufacturing, if the same part is manufactured at multiple locations around the globe, it is important to factor those considerations into the decision-making process. It may be difficult to ship certain standardized parts to a particular location. Perhaps there are local content laws or buying requirements that would negatively impact the overall benefits of the simplification in certain areas of the world.

In non-manufacturing, failure to take global requirements into consideration can have major implications for the business. Minor variations to a product or service in differing countries may serve cultural purposes, or have a specific local reason for existence.

The cross-functional team should include global members, and bring into consideration the ideas, opinions and requirements of the global business.

C)   **Applications**

1.0   **High-use or high-volume items** — High-volume items are good candidates for standardization. Also, parts and components that have a great deal of commonality should be considered for standardization. Since organizations generally implement contracted buying programs for high-use or high-volume parts, it is important to examine all contracts for any parts being considered for elimination or change to ensure the terms and conditions of the agreement and the forward buying plans are not negatively impacted by the decisions of the team.

2.0   **Procurement of facilities** — Many organizations in the service and manufacturing sectors have standardized their facilities so that the footprint or external shape of the facility is the same no matter where it is located. Others have standards regarding exterior and interior layout, requirements for certain safety and security standards, and number and placements of entrances and exits, as well as other requirements. When facilities or land for facilities are leased or purchased, it is important for supply professionals to see that the required standards can be implemented with the property or facility under consideration. Standardization of facilities can reduce overall costs of design, construction and training, among other costs.

3.0 **Procurement of MRO and indirect items** — Procurement of MRO and indirect supplies is a good starting place for any standardization program. Many of the items purchased for MRO are standardized by their very nature and therefore could be further reviewed to identify where further standardization would be effective.

4.0 **Procurement of services** — Both service and manufacturing organizations purchase services from other organizations on a regular basis. These purchased services may include consulting, legal, accounting, catering, custodial, building and equipment maintenance, transportation, landscaping, snow removal and uniform cleaning services, among others. A review of the total amount spent with each of these services may reveal that several business units within the organization are purchasing similar services from the same supplier, often at different rates for essentially the same service. One area of standardization involves the combination of contracts to receive the same rates throughout the organization, generate higher volume with the supplier and increase the supplier's awareness of the importance of the organization as their customer.

In addition, since these purchased services are generally not the core competencies of the organization, it is often a cost advantage to standardize the process of acquiring these services from one supplier, thus eliminating non-value-added activities. Organizations may consider standardizing the outsourcing of services to one organization to simplify the invoicing and payment processes, and to reduce the number of contacts and communication issues.

Organizations may purchase certain services that are a subset of the services provided by the organization in delivery of products and services to their ultimate customers. Transportation is a typical example, but the services purchased can be anything. In addition, the number and complexity of the types of service offerings purchased may involve many single-source or sole-source providers that cannot be standardized or simplified. In undertaking a standardization program, the team will need to do a thorough review of the types of services being purchased and how each particular service fits into the delivery of its own service to the ultimate customer.

D) **Brand names versus generic names** — One of the higher-level objectives for standardization and simplification programs is interchangeable parts. This is beneficial to the supplier, distributor and ultimately the purchaser of that part.

Specifications sometimes state a requirement for a brand name or equivalent. If the requirement states the specification in this manner, a component can be substituted for items that are equal to or better than the brand named item. It must be able to perform in the same "fit, form or function" that the brand named item would.

E) **Cost/benefit analysis** — A key component of a material standardization program is the cost/benefit analysis. A return on investment (ROI) model is typically used to review the cost associated with the cost avoidance and cost savings that are expected to be gained by pursuing the project. A total cost of ownership analysis may be a good way to determine whether the benefits outweigh the costs of a standardization project. If the benefits are greater than the costs, and the resources are available, the project or program is worth the pursuing. Total cost of ownership is discussed in Tasks 1-B-4, 3-C-4 and 3-C-5.

2) Sources of standards

There are many sources for identifying appropriate standardization goals for a project. The following list is by no means an exhaustive compilation of available resources to research, but provides some ideas and resources:

A) **Internal organization** — Internal work instructions, procedures and policies are sources the organization may use to assure the product is produced to a standard specification set by the business. In manufacturing environments, a quality manual is another document that will be available for review. Service industries frequently have standards for dress, behavior, communication with clients and customers, manner of delivery, products that may be used in conjunction with providing the service, and care of facilities and equipment.

Employee empowerment can be a powerful standardization tool. Letting the employee who is producing the product have input and ownership into the quality process has produced very successful results in the last decade.

B) **Government (for example, U.S. National Institute of Standards and Technology)** — Governments, domestic or international, often create standards that are mandatory or voluntary based on perceived needs or expected outcomes. Organizations need to recognize these standards and make accommodations accordingly.

In the United States, the National Institute of Standards and Technology (NIST), founded in 1901, is a nonregulatory federal agency within the U.S. Commerce Department's Technology Administration. NIST's mission is to promote innovation and industrial competitiveness by advancing measurement science, standards and technology in ways that enhance economic security and improve our quality of life. NIST sees one of its core competencies as helping business to develop and use standards in manufacturing. For more information on NIST, see www.nist.gov/.

In the United States, there are many other standards-setting and standards-enforcing agencies. Among them include the following:

- Food and Drug Administration (www.fda.gov/)

- Federal Aviation Administration (www.faa.gov/)

- Nuclear Regulatory Commission (www.nrc.gov/)

- U. S. Department of Agriculture (www.usda.gov/)

- Occupational Safety and Health Administration (www.osha.gov/).

European Standards Organizations include the European Committee for Standardization (CEN), European Committee for Electrotechnical Standardization (CENELEC) and the European Telecommunications Standards Institute (ETSI).

C) **International**

1.0 **International Organization for Standardization (ISO)** — The International Organization for Standardization has gained prominence with the increase of global outsourcing. ISO 9000 is a family of standards related to quality. Some of the best known standards include the following:

- ISO 9000 — Fundamentals and vocabulary

- ISO 9001 — Quality management systems

- ISO 9004 — Guidelines for performance improvements

- ISO 19011 — Guidelines for auditing quality.

More than 150 member countries participate in the ISO organization. The primary objective is to demonstrate that an organization is capable of controlling variances in its processes. A third-party registrar audits and awards registration to applicants that meet very stringent requirements. Maintaining a well managed quality management system is the key to being awarded ISO status.

Standards are set each year by the governing body. One current objective is the demonstration of management's involvement in continuous improvement. Being ISO-registered shows a level of competency to customers that the organization is capable of delivering manufacturing items. A supplier that is ISO certified is a good candidate to become a certified supplier. Some organizations will do business with ISO certified suppliers only. Other organizations have their own ISO like standards for a specific industry. An example is the automobile industry. ISO has released two environmental standards, ISO 14000 and 14001. ISO 17799 establishes guidelines for implementing an information security management system. ISO standard 17799 ensures the confidentiality and integrity of vital corporate and customer information. The ISO 28000 series is a set of standards that address the potential security issues at all stages of the procurement process, which target threats such as terrorism, fraud and piracy.

2.0 **United Nations Standard Products and Services Code (UNSPSC)** — It is important for supply management professionals to know how much organizations spend on what products from which suppliers. Savings opportunities are often missed due to inadequate spend analysis. Also, effective spend analysis enables supply professionals to better plan and budget, leverage volume purchases, enforce contract compliance and track supplier performance. The UNSPSC is a business tool that enables better spend analyses using a five-level hierarchical classification system for more than 20,000 categories of products and services. The system is available in ten languages.

D) **Industry/associations**

1.0 **American National Standards Institute (ANSI)** — While it does not directly impact a standardization project, supply management professionals should be aware of the American National Standards Institute (ANSI) as the organization that facilitates the voluntary setting of consensus standards and oversees their integrity. For example, ANSI governs U.S. electronic data interchange standards. For more information, see www.ansi.org/.

The standards are an agreement on definite characteristics of quality, design, performance, quantity or service. In the Internet world, a standard usually applies to an industrywide agreement of code or hardware linkages such as a hypertext markup language (HTML) or ANSI-X12.

2.0 **Institute for Electrical and Electronics Engineers (IEEE) —**
The primary purpose of IEEE is to foster technological innovation and excellence for the benefit of humanity. The Institute
develops and publishes industry standards for a wide range of
technologies which are available at its website. It provides a
good reference point for supply management professionals as
they seek out and review specifications of innovative products
and materials.

BIBLIOGRAPHY

Institute for Electrical and Electronics Engineers (IEEE). www.ieee.org,
March 2013.

International Organization for Standardization (ISO). www.iso.org, May 2013.

The United Nations. www.un.org, May, 2013.

United Nations Standard Products and Services Code (UNSPSC). www.unspsc.org,
March 2013.

Develop/implement a warehouse and inventory management system.

Organizations use inventory to improve their ability to coordinate supply with demand and control transportation and supply costs. The warehouse supports this effort and should be able to quickly locate stored inventory for shipment to the customer. Thus, there are a number of considerations in developing an effective and efficient warehouse and inventory management system.

1) Physical tracking systems

The supply management professional needs to understand the benefits and limitations of various physical tracking systems as well as the costs and procedures associated with using them. Physical tracking systems are a necessity for locating inventory items, and linking those items to an inventory or warehouse management system (WMS) helps to provide accurate and timely information for supply management and other management decisions. Customers such as the U.S. government and large retailers are placing stringent requirements on their suppliers to provide products that can be easily identified and tracked.

A) **RFID (radio frequency identification)** — Radio frequency identification devices/systems are being implemented by many organizations in a variety of ways. The primary components are the host computer, reader, interface transmitter and tag device. A passive or active radio data chip is attached to products to allow retailers to track, access and compile data as part of the supply chain flow process (ISM *Glossary* 2014). Tagless systems allow the "tag" to be printed directly on an item, which lowers costs. RFID may be used for individual items, entire cartons and containers as large as those used in ocean shipping. RFID systems are a strong tool for use with security information systems. RFID tags may be used to provide the manifest for shipping containers that have been sealed at the factory and whose contents have been verified. This verification and electronic manifest may allow the container to pass through customs security inspections at many ports with greater ease and speed than those containers not so identified. RFID tags are used in animal identification, media centers and libraries, hospitals, prepaid toll road passes and countless other applications. New applications are being proposed daily wherever information pertinent to a single item needs to be available or trackable.

The key benefit to RFID is that it maintains real-time communications on all inventory encompassed in the inventory system within range of the readers for the RFID system. This range may be from a few inches or centimeters to a much longer range. As the technology continues to develop, the ranges continue to increase. The RFID reader's function is to capture information remotely and transmit the data to the warehouse or inventory management system where it may be used for order and production planning, customer order fulfillment, replenishment decisions, order tracking or other purposes.

The initial cost to invest in all the components needed for an RFID system is sometimes expensive, but the cost is dropping as more systems are manufactured and used. Tagless systems reduce the cost and make wider use more feasible. Other areas of concern are data security, invasion of privacy and lack of current agreement on a single standard.

B) **Bar code** — Bar coding is an inventory control system that employs the use of codes that are machine readable. It allows for the easy identification of an organization's inventory and other assets such as equipment and furniture. The bar codes used are a pattern of parallel bars and spaces that represent specific characters and numbers. When a bar code is read by a scanning device, it interfaces with computerized records and allows for automatic updating of inventory records. The use of bar codes in the retail industry has been common for many years, as it reduces data entry errors while improving processing speed and inventory accuracy. The Universal Product Code (UPC) is a popular form of bar coding used extensively by retailers and the food and grocery industries. Bar coding has made those industries more efficient in receiving, inventory, warehouse management and reordering for replenishment, as well as sales management. One common application of bar codes is an intelligent shipping label. Within a small space, information can be stored and accessed, including purchase information, carrier code and freight-sort code. Bar codes have had an impact on supply chain management for more than three decades, increasing efficiency as well as the accuracy of records. A challenge with bar codes is that many industries have different standards (Stanley and Matthews 2014).

C) **UID — Unique Identification Device** —The Department of Defense, the U.S. Food and Drug Administration, the U.S. Patent Agency, other U.S. government agencies and several industries use a unique identification system which consists of a reader device (UID) to retrieve data encoded on machine-readable media. These systems are also known as Moveable Object Accountability Systems and are designed to identify and track unique objects. A UID system encodes data on an object. That data is typically in the form of an encoded data matrix and contains a unique identifier. It is a one-of-a-kind item identifier system of labeling objects. The best known application is by the Department of Defense (DoD). Any organization contracting with the U.S. government must be prepared to become familiar with a UID system (see http://www.infosight.com/uidtags.htm for more information).

Markings on items are labeled with an encoded data matrix. The data environment contains a unique item identifier. Goods that are encompassed in the system are items of interest to national security, classified and sensitive items, items costing more than $5,000, items furnished to a third party such as a contractor or any item over which tight control is necessary.

2) Overall project plan

As information technology and material handling technologies have improved, and security issues related to physical assets and data have increased, the need to manage inventories and warehouses well has become increasingly important. The need to provide high levels of customer service to remain competitive and to be a good customer to suppliers has driven enhancements in inventory and warehouse management systems. The supply management professional should be aware of how constantly changing technology can help the warehouse and inventory management systems add value for both internal and external customers.

A) **Plan for business continuity** — Business continuity and disaster recovery plans are strategic guiding principles of how to ensure an organization can maintain and continue operations in the face of unexpected crisis or disaster. Crises or disasters may range from those caused by humans — such as arson, robbery or terrorist attack, to a force of nature — such as tsunami, hurricane or earthquake. Organizations rely on continued generated revenue to survive. When operations are disrupted, recovery should be quicker if a plan for an approach to recovery is in place.

Business continuity is the sustaining of business operations in support of customer needs. Capabilities, communications and data must be maintained so that the finished product can get to the customer for the business to remain viable and profitable. Disaster recovery is being properly prepared for when a crisis seriously affects an organization. Both business continuity and disaster recovery are action plans that are enforced when a situation occurs that could affect the continuation of the business. The better an organization is prepared for this type of situation, the better the results will be in minimizing the risk of loss of life or assets as well as supply chain effectiveness.

Supply continuity is the provision for the continued receipt of supplies in the event of a disruption of normal supply chain channels, or a plan to prevent such disruption from occurring. Such a plan might include multiple production facilities, multiple suppliers, effective production and quality systems, along with disaster recovery plans. Supply may be disrupted for reasons other than those generated by the organization receiving the supply, and may be caused by the failure of another organization to engage in disaster or business continuity planning.

Internal and external supply chain business continuity plan and recovery plans for warehouse and inventory management supply interruptions typically include the following:

- Plans for employees' safety and escape from dangerous situations

- Methods of communicating with and locating employees during and after the disaster

- Communications for all stakeholders including employees, customers, suppliers, shareholders

- Plans for communicating with the press; a good recommendation is to have a designated spokesperson who tells the truth about what is known about the situation as it develops

- Regularly backing up data so that databases can be restored to a point just before the crisis or disaster, if necessary

- Contingent shipping methods

- Contingency plan for labor interruption

- Plans for safeguarding equipment, computer systems and other assets

- Action plans for escape paths

- Having well-developed supplier relationships

- Knowledge of alternative sources of supply

- Training for disasters that are likely to occur in the area in which the organization is located; earthquake training for employees if the business is in an area where earthquakes are common, or response to a robbery for bank employees are examples

- Generic disaster drills

- Maintaining safety stock level.

When a major business interruption or disaster occurs, it is helpful to have a defined strategy in place as well as plans for contingencies. The cost to plan is generally less than the cost of prolonged disruption.

B) **Implementation plan** — When planning an inventory management system, typical objectives include minimizing inventory-related risks and ensuring smooth operations as the costs of ordering and carrying inventory are balanced against the costs of stockouts. Key considerations for a warehouse management system plan include meeting customer requirements, cost considerations and the technologies available for warehouse management systems. Plans for both the inventory and warehouse management systems should fit within the overall strategy of an organization and should be integrated with each other. The two are not identical but should be thought of as overlapping circles. While it would be unlikely that an organization would need a warehouse if it had no inventory, it is quite possible to have inventory without having a physical warehouse. The overriding goal of either of these systems should be to add value for the customers, both internal and external.

When planning a change to inventory or warehouse management, or both, a good starting point is to describe the current state of affairs. One of the most powerful ways to perform this activity is to make a set of detailed process flow diagrams describing the current flows of materials and services into, through and out of the systems under consideration. Process flow diagrams will include quantities and timing of flows, when possible. The more details that are included, the better it is to understand the system and where improvements can and should be made. Users of the current systems should be consulted, as should independent observers. Recorded data should be compiled to support the process flow diagrams, and verification should be made that the resulting set of diagrams is a good representation of the processes under review.

Once the current states of the inventory and warehouse management systems are understood, it is usually easy to see where changes should be made and what the priorities should be. During the process of collecting data about the system, many will have shared objectives for what they hope a new system will do, so those objectives must be prioritized. Once that has been done, a system can be designed that will accommodate as many of those objectives as is feasible.

A transition plan to move from the current system to the new system must be designed, and a team put in place to lead the transition.

Transition milestones should be determined, and performance objectives set for the new systems such as product availability, inventory turnovers, throughput, order fill rate, stockouts, mishandled items, number of items received in a given time period, inventory accuracy, order filling accuracy and length of time to fill orders from their receipt. Determination of training needs and a plan for continuity of the business during the switchover are also important. It is important there be a budget for the plan. The funding available for the project will have a strong influence on what can be accomplished.

Overall measures at a strategic level should be set as some of the goals may relate to serving a larger geographic area, more facilities and/or more customers. The overriding goal of adding value for the customers should be kept in mind at all times, and the elimination of non-value-added steps from the processes should be a major objective.

C) **Manpower and equipment requirements** — Labor and equipment are the largest operating cost items in the warehouse budget. Floor space and cube warehouse space are the largest capital costs because of the investment in facilities. Electronic and computer systems and material handling systems are other large investments.

If labor rates are high, it may be possible to justify the cost of automated equipment. Having a warehousing system that is efficient and effective can be challenging if commodities being stored are constantly changing and equipment and/or training costs are always variable costs. Flexibility of a system to switch some portion of its operations between human resources and equipment is highly desirable.

D) **Facility design** — The objective of the facility design is to make sure the activities performed in the warehouse are adding value for one's customers, and are minimizing the non-value-added activities. A high level of efficiency and high utilization of labor, equipment and space are all desirable. Warehouses are usually divided into areas that perform different functions and processes. These areas are likely to include receiving, storage and shipping. Some warehouses are operated so that the dock area is a receiving area during one part of the day and a shipping area during another part of the day. There may be an area for cross-docking, inspection of goods, breaking bulk, special order pallet assembly, problem resolution, other assembly processes, and sometimes even production lines, depending on what services the warehouse performs to add value for customers.

The size of the warehouse will depend on its location relative to other warehouses, and whether it is a general purpose warehouse or has special requirements. Examples of special requirements are refrigeration or temperature control, a high level of security for items of high value or of a sensitive nature, storage of highly flammable items, or storage of hazardous or corrosive materials. Warehouses also might store fast moving goods in convenient locations. If items have expiration dates and must be stored so they can be retrieved on a first-in, first-out basis, this requirement must be considered in the upfront design. Sometimes shelves are designed so that new items are added from one side and picked from the other.

The design of the warehouse must facilitate how goods are received, stored and issued. Materials handling equipment and personnel needed are key factors influencing how the facility is designed. How the movement of materials is performed is another design consideration, including patterns needed for group picking, zone picking and commodity picking. Designers of a new facility must consider all the activities in each of the process areas.

Organizations may choose to expand a facility vertically, otherwise known as build up, or horizontally, referred to as build out. The height of the building will dictate how high shelving can be assembled, which is a key consideration in warehouse design. Higher shelf racking almost always allows for better space utilization. In addition to square footage (SF), it is important to consider cubage (cubage is the cubic volume of space being used or available for shipping or storage). Vertical capacity requirements relate directly to the type of equipment that will be needed.

E) **Physical constraints** — The characteristics of the goods stored create the physical constraints. These considerations are very similar to the cost considerations that need to be identified, such as the following:

- Type of goods

- Size and weight of the product stored

- Special equipment requirements

- Danger level of an accident

- Value of the goods stored

- Security requirements.

F) **Fixed or random storage locations** — Within a facility, two types of storage systems are typically used: fixed and random. A fixed location system is one that stores the inventory item in a set physical location. If an item is stored on a given shelf and bin location, it can always be found there. This method of storage usually has lower space utilization and higher accuracy. It also simplifies storing and record keeping.

Random location systems store inventory in any available space. As a rule, the use of random locations results in a higher utilization of space, but lower accuracy. More analysis of real-time data is required to know if spaces are empty or can be consolidated. However, there is a higher utilization of cubic space than with the fixed system.

In either system, the warehouse location of material is identified in the perpetual inventory record. Ultimately, supply management must ensure that the needed materials get to the customer. Therefore, supply management professionals need to be aware of how materials can be stored and how quickly they can be accessed. RFID increases the advantages of random storage because accuracy of the information system is improved.

3) Customer requirements

Adding value for customers, both internal and external, should be the driving force in the development and implementation of inventory management and warehouse management systems. Customer requirements may vary widely based on the following:

- Frequency of order placement

- Size of orders in terms of quantity and in monetary terms

- Variety of items in an order

- Methods by which the order may be shipped or delivered

- Amount of processing needed to prepare the order

- Special requirements or handling of some or all of the items in the order (temperature, fragility or partial assembly)

- Packaging requirements (small carton that may be placed directly on the shelf, small individualized portions, large carton that will be broken down by the customer or formation of special pallets with a variety of items)

- Security requirements (controlled substances, hazardous materials, items of high value).

For example, a hospital pharmacy may deliver medications from its inventory to patients' rooms several times a day. Each patient is likely to have a unique set of medications prescribed. Mistakes in product identification, quantity, timing of delivery or labeling can be fatal. The pharmacist acts as the inventory manager and may place frequent orders with the hospital's drug representatives so as to have the correct drugs on hand in small packages, but not so much to have an oversupply on hand. The pharmacist also supervises the dispensing of the medications. In a sense, a pharmacist is a supply management professional who may not even be aware of it.

At the other end of the spectrum, larger retailers such as Target or Wal-Mart may require truckload deliveries of single or a few items from their suppliers at some regular frequency or at a pre-assigned time. As the contents are unloaded, they are immediately moved across the dock and broken down into specific smaller quantities, often in packaging that can go directly onto the shelves. These items are grouped with other items that came in by truckloads that have been similarly reduced in bulk. New pallets with a variety of products may be built, and identical pallets are loaded onto several trucks, each of which is going to a specific store. A retailer generally purchases a variety of items from one supplier. For example, Wal-Mart may purchase an assortment of personal care items from Procter & Gamble (P&G) that come out of a single P&G warehouse. Wal-Mart will ask P&G to form the pallets at P&G with the pre-assigned variety Wal-Mart requires before shipping to Wal-Mart. This makes Wal-Mart's cross-docking procedure even quicker and easier.

Many large organizations that ship to customers daily have outsourced part or all of their inventory management or warehouse management systems to organizations that describe themselves as third-party logistics suppliers (3PL). By outsourcing this function, the organization may save on labor and facilities costs and can use the leveraging capabilities of the 3PL provider to possibly reduce transportation costs. There are also organizations called 4PLs that manage groups of 3PLs for organizations.

Many businesses have arrangements with suppliers in which items that are needed by many departments, such as office suppliers, may be ordered by individual departments, charged to the corporate account, and delivered by the supplier within a specified (usually short) time frame. Some customers require that the supplier always hold other types of inventory that can be delivered within a designated time frame.

The supply management professional is challenged to be ever more creative and flexible in determining how value can be added for the customer while balancing the need to make a profit.

4) Cost considerations

Customers today want their goods stored, physically managed and delivered with a minimal cost and a high level of service. Some warehouse contracts are based on floor space cost only. If a warehouse can perform services that add value for the customer, those services should be more attractive to the customer and may allow the warehouse to earn a higher margin on such services. For example, a warehouse may add value by unpacking a container and repackaging the goods in a configuration that is used directly at the production line or on the store shelf. The activity should be accepted by the warehouse (and the customer) only if both can increase profits by the change; in other words, the customer can reduce operating costs enough to cover the warehouse costs while providing a marginal profit to the warehouse for providing the service.

There are numerous costs involved in warehouse management that should be considered by supply management professionals. Some relate to the customer requirements; the nature of the customers; the products stored; the warehouse design, layout and structure; the equipment used and the personnel required.

Examples of characteristics that can affect cost include the following:

- Type of products stored

- Variety of the products stored

- Specific requirements for safety, security, temperature, shelf life

- Size and weight of the products stored

- Special equipment requirements

- Special requirements related to the products (may relate to temperature, flammability, legal requirements such as controlled substances, safety and security)

- Safety, security and training requirements for warehouse personnel

- Value of the products stored

- State of automation of the warehouse

- Size of the warehouse

- Location of the warehouse

- Physical structure of the warehouse

- Ownership arrangement (leased or owned, wholly or in part)

- Communications systems available

- Flexibility, availability, skill set and location of the labor pool

- Customer expectations

- Quality standards enforced or required.

There are others, including those based on level of service or location.

Considering these characteristics can assist in managing the costs by implementing process changes and improvements.

5) Available technology for warehouse management system (WMS)

A) **SWOT analysis** — Analyzing the strengths, weaknesses, opportunities and threats (SWOT) of a warehouse management system (WMS) is similar to performing a SWOT analysis on the decision to acquire, enhance or upgrade any information management system for an organization. A SWOT analysis is among many tools that may be used in the strategic planning process. A SWOT analysis might be particularly useful in warehouse decisions, such as questions about whether to lease or own, how many warehouses are needed, where to locate the warehouses, what product variety to manage in each, or what value-added services to offer. There are several commercially available software tools that will assist in performing a SWOT analysis. Such an analysis may be performed without computer assistance by brainstorming with a group of knowledgeable supply management professionals and other appropriate team members. The concept is to reach consensus on the strengths, opportunities, weaknesses and threats for a given organization under certain circumstances. The results are examined and a list of several different courses of action are proposed regarding how to capitalize on strengths, shore up weaknesses, take advantage of opportunities and thwart threats. Ultimately a set of recommendations is proposed by those performing the SWOT analysis that may or may not be the final decision-makers.

There are specific tools in some WMS software solutions that analyze and help identify a focus for the core competencies of a given business. To perform a SWOT analysis using WMS software (or any software), it is necessary to input the internal strengths and weakness and the external opportunities and threats for the situation. However, the software in some circumstances can help with the analysis, point out trade-offs that may not be obvious, and propose a list of alternatives — and perhaps propose a feasible solution. It is unlikely that the SWOT analysis module of a warehouse management system is the core strength of the WMS.

Warehouse management systems have evolved over the years from their initial focus on management of flows into and out of warehouse and storage locations. As with all information management technology over the past several decades, warehouse management systems have morphed into performing a wide variety of tasks while still maintaining their basic abilities. Here are some of the features and functionality that a supply management professional should look for in a warehouse management system:

- A flexible location assignment system

- The ability for the user to define parameters for the tasks at hand (such as use of FIFO or LIFO for picking)

- Easy-to-use integration with data collection devices, including bar code scanners and RFID technology

- Reasonable logic in determining locations and put-away or picking sequences.

- Various order-picking choices such as wave, batch or zone picking

- The ability to interweave tasks (such as put-away and pick)

- Automated data collection

- Cycle counting

- Labor tracking and capacity planning

- Integration with accounting and enterprise resource planning systems

- The ability to communicate with WMS at other locations belonging to the organization itself, or to its customers or suppliers.

A SWOT analysis involving affected parties will help define the most important features to consider.

6) Warehouse management

A) **Structures** — One important warehouse management goal is to minimize the cost associated with the storing, movement and transportation of goods into and out of the warehouse stores location. This cost minimization must be accomplished while providing the best possible customer service and making the best use of space, labor and equipment.

There are two primary types of warehouse structures. One is characterized by private ownership and the other by leased or outsourced warehousing services, typically called public warehousing. One organization may choose to use both types of structures for its warehousing needs, depending on the location, volume, product characteristics and services desired. For example, an organization may choose privately owned warehousing, but also lease public warehouse space at peak times, or in geographic locations where the organization's product volume does not warrant its own warehouse.

A manufacturing organization or a large retail organization may choose to own its own warehouses or distribution centers (DCs). Such a choice creates a fixed cost on the income statement (depreciation expense) and a fixed asset on the balance sheet. For an organization for which warehouse or DC management is not a core competency, high labor costs and lower efficiencies can result. A possible trade-off is better control and better customer service. Organizations that have become experts at managing large distribution centers, such as Target, Wal-Mart and Amazon, have found the trade-offs in favor of ownership to be positive. Many distribution center innovations over the past two decades, such as cross-docking and the use of RFID, have come from these retail giants.

Public warehousing has numerous sub-structures. Short-term or long-term leases of warehouses and related services that are owned and operated by other than the contracting organization are referred to as outside service. It has become common to hire a separate organization that specializes in warehousing and transportation services to manage those functions for an organization for which warehousing and transportation management are not core competencies. Organizations that manage a variety of logistics services for other organizations are called third-party logistics organizations, which are often abbreviated as 3PL services. 3PL organizations offer a menu of items from which their customers may choose. Some 3PL organizations own their own assets, and others lease the services and assets of yet another layer of suppliers. The latter structure allows the 3PL organization great flexibility in meeting its customers' needs. For an organization that uses public warehousing or 3PL services, these costs now become pre-tax expenses in the income statement. Depending on the type of leasing arrangement, these arrangements are likely to have no effect on the asset and liability sections of the balance sheet of the leasing organization.

Customer service is a key performance indicator in the performance measurements for private or public warehousing and use of 3PL services.

In a global environment, organizations may contract with 3PLs not only to fill their warehouses needs but also to perform supplier-managed inventory functions for them. A 3PL may be held responsible for inventory replenishment, and may take the inventory on consignment so that it is on the balance sheet of the 3PL. When the goods are sold, the 3PL will forward payment from the customer to the manufacturer.

Centralized and decentralized structures may be used in both the private and public warehousing environments.

In a centralized warehouse system, order replenishment decisions are made in one location. The requirements of the entire distribution and warehouse network are combined. A major benefit of the centralized system is that total customer service and demand needs are balanced through the system. Another advantage of centralized replenishment decision-making is that volume purchasing can be used to create larger cost savings. Disadvantages are that decisions are sometimes delayed and do not always take into consideration the individual needs of one individual location. If the inventory must be transshipped to other locations, transportation costs may be higher than in a decentralized system.

In a decentralized warehouse system, each location functions independently from all others in the system. Advantages of a decentralized system are that decisions can be made faster and are more closely matched to the customers' demand from a given site. Disadvantages are the higher costs associated with smaller orders and more overall inventory in the system.

B) **Storage location** — Warehouse management systems (WMS) frequently have computer programs that will attempt to optimize stocking locations for incoming goods. These programs are usually based on multiple objectives in which some of the goals include the following:

- Minimize stocking costs

- Minimize picking costs

- Maximize space usage

- Group similar items as closely together as possible

- Ensure that all constraints with respect to safety, temperature and security are met

- Put away and pick on a timely basis

- Provide good customer service.

In spite of many computer and mathematical models, there is no perfect stocking location method. If optimum efficiency is ever achieved, it is disturbed every time there is a new receipt of goods or an order is picked. Since these events happen with great regularity, there are algorithms that attempt to achieve these objectives, but there still are many variables. Each type of commodity or good has unique characteristics and must be configured according to its characteristics and the projected needs for the item.

Examples of locations:

- Fixed items are stored at permanent location(s) dedicated to hold only that item. Fixed location(s) can be reassigned if the part stored becomes obsolete or the demand shifts significantly and more or less space is needed. These locations are usually chosen with a goal of minimizing the put-away, storage and picking costs, as well as meeting the other physical constraints for the goods. However, the space utilization may not be as high as with a random system.

- Random/floating locations are implemented for goods that must be stored at multiple locations. These goods usually have a high inventory turn, thus the locations can be temporarily assigned for different items in high demand. The benefit of this type of location is cube utilization and warehouse efficiency.

- Overflow locations are used when more inventories than expected come into the warehouse. Overflow locations are always considered temporary. Goods should be pulled from these overflow location on a last-in, first-out (LIFO) basis to be able to free up space for the storage of other goods. Items in overflow locations may be moved to regular random or fixed locations within the warehouse when the overflow need has subsided.

- Point-of-use locations within the warehouse are usually managed by a visual Kanban method. Point-of-use locations are used to store goods close to the consumption area and replaced on a pull signal only when demand is required. Point-of-use locations are likely to be used when the warehouse provides assembly services.

C) **Replenishment systems** — Distribution requirements planning (DRP) is a time-based demand from the distribution center to balance the customer fill rate against inventory investment (ISM *Glossary* 2014). It uses a time-phased order point to determine when a quantity of goods must be planned and received. It is the primary method of planning goods in a warehouse management system. DRP is an information system that takes individual customer demands on a set of warehouses or distribution centers projected over the next several periods of time, and uses that information to predict demand across the warehouses. This information, along with information about current warehouse inventory, is sent back to the manufacturing information system, specifically to the master production schedule, to determine when items must be replenished. Thus, a DRP system links customers, distribution centers, warehouses and manufacturing plants to help an organization plan its flows of materials.

Kanban replenishment is a "lean" concept approach to warehouse management. Lean concepts focus on minimization of inventory while maximizing product flow. When using Kanban, inventory or materials are replaced only when there is a demand for those goods. Kanban is a Japanese term meaning "signal." It is usually a printed card that contains specific information such as part name, description, quantity and so on that signals a cycle of replenishment for production and materials. It is an order-release mechanism and is among the primary tools of a just in time (JIT) manufacturing system (ISM *Glossary* 2014).

D) **Inventory classification systems** — Inventory is frequently classified based on cost and demand patterns in which high value items in high demand receive the highest rating and require the most attention in terms of management. At the opposite end of the spectrum are items with low value and low demand that do not require as much attention from the supply management professional. A very common inventory classification system that has been in use for many years is the ABC inventory classification system. (Please note this form of inventory classification is NOT related to Activity-Based Costing used in accounting systems.) The ABC inventory classification system is based on the premise that 20 percent of the items held in inventory for resale will generate 80 percent of the sales revenue. If the inventory items being analyzed are being held for use in production or assembly, then approximately 20 percent of the items will generate 80 percent of the cost of items being used. The inventory items are sorted as to sales revenue generated (or value of items used) and the top 20 percent are called "A" items. The next 30 percent of the items are classified as "B" items, and will usually generate about 15 percent of the revenue (or cost), and the last 50 percent of the items will generate about 5 percent of the sales or cost. After items are classified, the "A" items should receive tight control as it is critical not to run out of these items. Forecasts should be done carefully, and safety stock levels should be analyzed to make certain they are not too high or too low. Special attention should be paid to lead time. Inventory accuracy is very important for these items. Classification is of interest to supply management professionals as it may be advantageous to set up supplier managed inventory (SMI), easy replenishment methods, centralized purchasing or quantity discounts with frequent delivery. "B" items are important but probably do not need to be reviewed as frequently. "C" items may be more loosely controlled. One of the criticisms of this method is that a "B" or "C" item may be a critical part that is not often needed but will stop operations if it is out of stock. One method to manage such a situation is to identify those items and either manage the spares carefully or have rapid replenishment plans in place. This classification method and how to manage items in "B" and "C" categories is further discussed in Stanley and Matthews, *Effective Supply Management Performance*, ISM *Professional Series* 2014.

Other ways that inventory can be classified are based on the type of materials, the characteristics of the items, size or shelf life, and methods of receiving, storing and issuing the goods. Any goods that have an associated hazard must be handled, stored and managed by specially trained personnel. Goods that require any special method of movement, storing and handling must be segregated and may require special attention from the supply management professional.

E) **Perpetual** — A perpetual inventory review system is an inventory control record system that requires immediate recording of transactions (receipts and withdrawals) for each item carried in inventory. If posted accurately, the inventory records are up-to-date and should agree with the actual stock count in the warehouse (ISM *Glossary* 2014). The perpetual system is sometimes called a continuous-review system because the status of inventory is checked after every transaction. In theory, the inventory records are updated with every transaction. For example, daily receipts may be batched and recorded one time each day, at the same time each day. If posted accurately, the inventory records are always up-to-date and should agree with the actual stock count in the warehouse. The use of a perpetual inventory system does not negate the need for physical inventory counts. However, if employees are well trained, good control procedures are in effect, transactions are convenient to record, updating of the database is automatic, and computer failures are few, then the data should be accurate and should very closely match the stock level in the warehouse. In terms of reordering items, a perpetual inventory system checks the status of inventory after each transaction to see if the level has fallen below the reorder point. If so, an order of a predetermined size is placed. One of the functions of supply management professionals using this type of system is to set the reorder parameters and the order quantity so that holding and order costs are minimized, and stockouts do not occur during lead time. In a perpetual system, the order quantity is of a fixed size, but the time between orders varies with the rate of usage of the item.

Accurate inventory information is important as numerous departments that include supply management, production planning, customer service, transportation and finance can use this information for advanced planning.

An alternative system called the periodic inventory review system records completed transactions in batches. The ISM *Glossary* 2014 defines the periodic system as a fixed-order interval inventory control system in which an item's inventory position is reviewed on a scheduled periodic basis, rather than continuously. An order is placed at the end of each review, if appropriate, and the order quantity usually varies. This system is different from a fixed-order quantity system in which the order quantity typically is fixed and the time between orders varies. The system is updated on a certain established date or time. For example, it may be updated every night at midnight, or once a week on Sunday morning, or at the end of every month, or some other established time period. There are few non-computerized inventory systems in the developed world, although some small businesses may still operate with inventory records kept by hand.

The role of the supply management professional is to set the parameters for the time between reviews, and the "order-up-to" level. In other words, if the order-up-to level is set at 500 and the inventory position is 325 when the periodic review takes place, an order for 175 units will be placed. The order-up-to level determination takes into account the lead time for the item and the amount of safety stock desired.

Another use of a periodic system is when parts are not considered issued from inventory into production until the product has reached a certain point in the process. At that point, all parts in the product are considered as having been removed from inventory, and the system is periodically updated to include those parts that have become part of finished or partially finished products.

7) Inventory accuracy and inventory integrity

Many supply management professionals and others must know inventory levels so that purchases, production and distribution can be planned. Accurate knowledge of inventory levels and rates of usage improve forecast accuracy and are helpful in sharing information with suppliers about what orders might be expected over the next month, quarter or year.

Inventory integrity is equally important, as users of the inventory items must know that those items that appear to be available are in shape to be used, have not been damaged or have not become obsolete. The importance of physical counts are discussed earlier in this section, but one of the purposes of doing physical tallies of inventory is to ensure that shrinkage is not occurring at an unexpected rate, and to take steps to stop such shrinkage if it is happening.

A) **Stock-keeping unit (SKU) establishment** — Stock-keeping unit (SKU) is an individual unit or product that is stocked at a specific storage facility (ISM *Glossary* 2014). A unique number or bar code differentiates each SKU. At some point, each SKU or individual item may have its own RFID tag which will also act as a unique identifier in differentiating each item. All organizations must determine which items, or SKUs, are to be kept in inventory. This determination should be made after reviewing a number of factors that include customer preferences, industry trends, product cost, sales forecasts, profitability and storage capacity.

Creating SKUs for individual items is the initial step in identifying and controlling inventory. Some SKUs have meaningful numbers that will help personnel identify the items. Example 1 shows a part number that a trained inventory manager would find meaningful.

Example 1: PHW-125-2303
PHW - Purchased Commodity-Hardware
125 - Supplier identification
2303 - Supplier part number

In a non-meaningful SKU classification, the number assigned to the part does not have any relationship to the physical characteristics of the part. In this case, a number such as S1274043725 might be assigned to a part.

For example, an airline may assign reservation confirmation numbers that later become the passenger's unique boarding pass number. These identifiers — which may consist of letters and numbers — are assigned randomly, but no two passengers have the same number.

Debit and charge cards have unique identifiers that are in essence an SKU. The numbers on these cards may describe the issuing organization and have numbers unique to the cardholder.

RFID tags are used in many situations where unique identification is necessary. There are applications in animal science, health care and passports. There will continue to be RFID developments in any industry where accuracy and quick processing time are highly desirable.

B) **Physical inventory** — Warehouse inventory for a manufacturing organization is categorized as if it were held in a manufacturing plant or other environment. Physical inventory is classified as raw material, work in process, finished goods and inventory held for maintenance, repairs and operations (MRO items). There are sub-classifications such as repair parts or spares, excessive items, obsolete items and possible non-inventory items like office and building supplies.

In a retail distribution center, most inventory is held as finished goods. In some cases, inventory may require final assembly, or need to be kitted before sending to the customer. RFID technology has made it easier to track physical inventory and has improved inventory accuracy.

C) **Cycle counting** — Cycle counting, as defined in the ISM *Glossary*, is a physical stock checking system in which the inventory is divided into groups that are physically counted at predetermined intervals, depending on their ABC classification. Thus, the physical inventory counting goes on continuously without interrupting operations or storeroom activities; also referred to as "continuous inventory." The primary goal in cycle counting is to identify error-causing effects on inventory inaccuracies. It is an effective method of measuring the level of inventory accuracy. The process for cycle counting is to count certain part numbers or categories of items on a frequency equal to the level of importance of the item. This process is done by trained supply management personnel, usually the same people who are storing and issuing the goods. Cycle counting is usually scheduled during off shifts or slower work periods.

Goods may be classified using the ABC classification described in the previous section. This classification, based on annual usage multiplied by the item's value, is used to determine the frequency of physical counting.

The entire inventory may be classified into three classes:

- "A" Items: 20 percent of the items accounting for 80 percent of the total dollar usage; counting once a month.

- "B" Items: 30 percent of the items accounting for 15 percent of the total dollar usage; counting four times a year.

- "C" Items: 50 percent of the items accounting for 5 percent of the total dollar usage; counting once a year.

Inventory corrections are achieved through the cycle counting function; however, this should be an outcome of the function, not the objective. The primary objective is to identify the reasons, find the cause of any inaccuracies and correct the cause. If proper training and discipline are in place, high inventory accuracy should be achievable.

Cycle counting and the ABC inventory classification system are also discussed in the previous section.

D) **Reconciliation** — Once an inventory item has been counted and compared against the perpetual records, there may be a discrepancy. These variances are normally noted on discrepancy reports. Significant variances that are noted will warrant attention and often result in a recheck of the item and its quantity. Settling and resolving these variances is known as reconciliation. To reconcile the inventory records, an adjustment will be required. These reports will also serve as an audit trail for the warehouse (Stanley and Matthews 2014).

Another form of reconciliation is to compare open orders at suppliers with released orders from customers, both external and internal. These open orders should match. If they do not, discrepancies must be resolved. This function may be known as records management. The purpose of records management is to systematically control the records of orders from the creation of the documentation or receipt of the order through the processes of production, assembly, distribution, maintenance and retrieval to disposition.

E) **Shrinkage** — Shrinkage is the reduction in inventory that occurs when items are lost, stolen or misplaced. It may occur naturally through evaporation, age or expiration of shelf life. During certain production processes there may be a loss of materials due to the nature of the process. For example, in cutting, burring, sawing or drilling processes, material is removed from parts by design. It is incumbent on the product design and engineering team to make every attempt to keep that type of shrinkage to a minimum. However, it is often unavoidable. It may fall to supply management to find alternative uses for the scrap resulting from these processes.

Yield loss is a form of shrinkage. Yield may be defined as the ratio of usable output to input, when measured in the same terms. Yield loss occurs in processes, especially those in which a batch of items is processed together, in which not all output may be perfect, or when all items may not function at the highest desirable level. This is especially true in the manufacturing of microchips. Another example is from the dairy industry. Raw milk may start with inputs measuring 500 gallons, but as it passes through the processes of pasteurization, fat removal and homogenization, the output may measure 300 gallons. Thus, the yield would be 60 percent.

Yield losses of materials or inventory may be calculated and planned in the process, and should be carefully accounted for. Enterprising supply professionals often find uses for scrap resulting from yield losses.

F) **Issue/return** — A common term used in conjunction with "issue and return" is "store." The term "store" refers to keeping the item in a given location until there is a request for its use. The steps involved with storing inventory are receiving, issuing a paper or electronic record, determining a storage location and putting the item away in the designated location.

The terms "issue" and "return" refer to inventory going out of or coming into the warehouse.

The steps normally involved with issuing inventory are picking, staging and delivery. Upon a request from an internal user, perhaps the sales department, a paper or electronic pick ticket is generated in the warehouse identifying the materials needed. The item is then retrieved, or picked, from wherever it resides in the warehouse and staged for the customer. Staging can be a separate area of the warehouse where materials are housed until they are delivered or picked up.

Returns can occur for a variety of reasons. Perhaps more material was received than was needed or an incorrect item was received. If a customer returns material to the warehouse, proper procedures must be in place to inspect the item to ensure its condition and to adjust the inventory count. Since a return generates additional costs in labor time and handling, many organizations require a restocking fee. It is not unusual for a customer to pay 20 percent of the original purchase price to return an item. The customer may return damaged or unusable stock and will expect credit for the item. These items should not be returned to stock but should be properly disposed of and removed from the accounting and inventory records. Sometimes it is not easy to determine when and where in the supply chain the damage occurred, and contentious litigation may result. To accept a return and issue credit for it often requires a returning materials authorization (RMA).

These activities can occur at all stages of a production or assembly process and at all levels of inventory, including raw materials, work-in-process and finished goods.

In a pull environment, such as a just in time inventory system, materials are not issued until there is a demand requesting the materials. In a push environment, the materials are delivered to the next operation regardless of the demand for the item. A push environment occurs when goods are made to stock; this type of environment can be used in other situations as well.

All store, issue and return transactions must be recorded properly to assure that inventory accuracy is maintained.

G) **Recoup** — In inventory management, "recoup" describes a strategy that supply management professionals should have in place to recover losses in inventory and other assets when disposal is necessary due to obsolescence or damage. Inventory investment loss and recoupment of as much of the loss as possible are part of a strategic risk management plan. Organizations sometimes sell a new product at a price that does not cover all marginal costs because sale of the product will lead to sales of a supporting product at a full and profitable price. For example, printers may be sold at very low prices, because the manufacturers of the printers know that users will have to buy the printer ink cartridges at full price to keep using the printer. Sometimes the cartridges must be purchased at a cost to the consumer that is higher than the original cost of the printer. When marketing new products, forecasting an inventory investment loss can be calculated based on the offset of the cost associated with the total financial return of the sales. For example, when electronic game manufacturers market and sell a new product, they may sell it for less than the target cost of break-even operating cost. It is not unusual for electronic console makers to lose money on the game console itself, expecting to make up for the loss by selling multiple games to the end user later. Many organizations have used this type of strategy to introduce new products and recover their cost by selling the supporting goods.

Recouping the loss of as much as possible of excessive and obsolete inventory is a standard inventory management practice. Most organizations examine demand for items in the previous 12 months and study the forecast for demand in the upcoming 12 months. If there is no demand for a specific item or class of items, any inventory on hand for those items will be classified as surplus, excessive or obsolete. Some of the methods of recouping inventory losses include:

- Sell excessive inventory back to the supplier.

- Re-engineer the component for use elsewhere in the product's bill of material (BOM).

- Rework the item as an alternative part that is useable.

- Send it to a spare parts distribution center or another division if it is useful as a spare part or still needed elsewhere. This action will result in a transaction in the inventory management system although it will not change the immediate ownership of the unneeded parts in terms of the overall organization.

- Donate the items to a nonprofit organization that can use them and obtain a possible tax deduction.

- Sell the items at scrap value.

- Scrap at no value. Sometimes there is a cost to scrap an item or dispose of it properly, so this action may result in negative cash outflow to the organization.

The objective of elimination of the items is to obtain as much value as possible from the transaction. Any of these methods will remove the items from the financial assets on the balance sheet and avoid the carrying cost associated with holding the inventory. Supply management professionals are likely to find themselves involved in these decisions, gathering information and performing analyses of tradeoffs between options, and may also be in charge of executing the final plan.

H) **Inventory consolidation** — In recent years, private and public organizations have worked toward maintaining a leaner inventory. These efforts include reducing the amount and types of inventory on hand, as well as consolidating inventories at multiple locations. Another way organizations save is by reducing their safety stock. Inventory usage may be consistent, but fewer sites mean less overall safety stock (Stanley and Matthews 2014).

With multiple locations, lead times for each facility can vary, even for the same product. This type of decentralization can make forecasting requirements challenging. According to Evers and Beier (1998), when selecting the appropriate facility for consolidating inventory, a key consideration includes which site has the lowest average lead time (Stanley and Matthews 2014).

Consolidation of inventory occurs when considering location, freight, and staging or kitting of materials. The transactions associated with these movements are the keys to inventory accuracy and integrity. Accurate inventory transactions and continuously checking for accuracy at each of the locations is essential.

Global logistics and the transportation of goods internationally are costly. Containerization is the primary mode of transporting. It is highly desirable to work with international suppliers to pack containers in such a way that space is used as wisely as possible, that no more containers must be shipped by vessel than is necessary and that freight is consolidated to minimize logistics costs. Containerized goods are then moved from suppliers to a shipping terminal, where they sometimes are combined with similar shipments from other suppliers and prepared for shipment.

Sometimes a manufacturing site purchases goods from local suppliers and will use what is called a "milk run" to pick up goods. A truck that is owned by the purchaser or is a joint venture among the suppliers is used to pick up goods from several suppliers and deliver them to the customer. If the same group of suppliers has several common customers, the process may be expanded to include not only pick up from several suppliers but delivery to several customers.

These types of strategic consolidations are classified as freight consolidation.

Staging or kitting is another form of consolidation. The physical movements of materials from the storing area to a staging area and then to the consumption or shipping area are detailed in the sequencing and routing function. Goods are picked from one area, consolidated with other goods and then moved to the appropriate area. Sometimes these activities are carried out inside the stockroom by picking parts and staging them for production or shipping orders.

Location consolidation occurs when items with similar characteristics are received, stored and issued together. An example of location consolidation would be a reduction in distribution centers from one in every state in the contiguous United States and one in every European country, and consolidate to just two (one serving the western United States and one serving the eastern United States), and two that serve all of the European Union.

I)   **Security** — Access to inventory must be limited to ensure that inventory items and materials do not get lost, stolen, misplaced or damaged.

Anyone not responsible for the handling and movement of goods stored should not have access to those goods. The warehouse, storage locations and any location in which goods are stored should be off limits to all personnel except those who work in that area.

Procedures must be established for placing new items into inventory, receiving goods, requesting materials, and picking and releasing materials to the requestors or to the factory floor. These procedures must be recorded at each step using the appropriate tools in the inventory management systems. It is important to keep track of where materials are and to whom they have been released for further processing, movement or shipment elsewhere. Records must be updated automatically or by hand. Bar coding or RFID tags can be very useful in the updating process. A high level of inventory accuracy goes hand-in-hand with good security. Order placement systems are often linked directly to inventory management systems so that all related systems can be updated at the same time. These systems may be linked to customers and suppliers for ease of managing several stages of inventory, and projecting completion dates for orders. If items are removed from inventory to be used by employees, such as research or design engineers or others, it remains equally important to record the destination and responsible party for the checkout of the materials. When items are returned to inventory, independent of the source of the return, it is important to inspect the items for completeness before returning them to stock.

C-TPAT, the Customs Trade-Partnership Against Terrorism, was discussed in Task 2-B-3, 7. Through this initiative, the U.S. Customs and Border Protection Service asks that businesses ensure the integrity of their security practices and communicate their security guidelines to their business partners (importers, carriers, brokers, warehouse operators, manufacturers) within the supply chain. Many other countries are imposing similar requirements, such as the United Kingdom and Canada. In addition, the International Organization for Standardization (ISO) has issued ISO 28000 series, which is a series of standards on supply chain security management systems.

Another security requirement that may change terms and conditions for many shippers is the requirement that an organization importing goods in containers from a country outside the U.S. will be responsible for the goods from the time the container leaves the factory where the goods are produced. In the past, organizations often would not take responsibility for containers of goods until they passed ship's rail. RFID can be a useful tool in meeting this requirement. A representative of the buying organization for the goods leaving the factory can use RFID to attest to the manifest, which is an itemization of the items included in a particular shipment along with related details, for a particular container.

As cartons, pallets or other units of inventory are loaded, an exact description of the volume and weight of each carton or pallet can be made. The dimensions and weight of items placed in the shipping container can be compared with the dimensions and weight of the container to eliminate the possibility of false ends or floors or ceilings in the container that might be carrying contraband (drugs, weapons, other illegal cargo, even human beings). With use of RFID, the weight and other dimensions of the prescribed contents can be accurately recorded and compared with what they are expected to be. After it is determined there is no contraband, the container can be sealed until it reaches its destination. Containers that meet these requirements of pre-inspection can move through customs and inspections at many locations more quickly.

J) **Inventory policies/procedures** — The efficient and effective operation of any business function requires sound policies and procedures. Inventory management is no exception. The supply professional must play a key role in the development of an organization's inventory policies, which must have the support and buy-in of senior management. Policies should be easily understood by customers and staff, and should be reviewed and updated periodically (Stanley and Matthews 2014).

The importance of a well-developed policy manual for the warehouse should not be underestimated. It provides a blueprint for the entire organization on its supply management practices and reflects the value of the warehouse operation. World-class organizations inevitably have sound policies and procedures regarding inventory management. While each operation is unique, there are certain areas that must be addressed in warehouse policies and procedures or in the inventory management manual. These include safety, recycling, standardization, security and access to inventory. Policies should be in place and employees educated in proper procedures for inventory issuance, product returns, surplus property, inventory counting and requests for new inventory items. Distribution and delivery policies, procedures and targets should be set and understood, as well (Stanley and Matthews 2014).

Inventory accuracy and inventory integrity are best controlled by performing regular and routine training for all supply management personnel involved with handling the inventory. Establishing strict policies, holding people accountable for their errors and taking disciplinary action when errors are identified is essential.

Inventory policies and procedures should be periodically evaluated for effectiveness and cost. The trade-off between the two should be analyzed to ensure the effectiveness of a policy is worth the return on investment of implementation and ongoing costs.

Examples of some of these policies include:

- Safety and security — This has become of utmost concern. Periodic checks of the effectiveness of training of warehouse and inventory management personnel in safety and security procedures, as well as drills and reviews of concepts and procedures, may be necessary to maintain good safety and security records. Employees should be recognized and rewarded for longstanding safety and security records. The trade-offs for these costs of training, drills, review and recognition are the cost of one or more breaches of safety or security.

- Inventory accuracy in cycle counting procedures — This is used when cycle counters are performing the function and come across a discrepancy in a transaction. The policy regarding inventory accuracy should clarify the monetary value above which supervisory approval is required in order to make the correction. For high-value items, adjustments — either positive or negative — should be checked by supervisory personnel for all possible options for resolution.

- Allowable tolerance for adjusting low-level C items during cycle counting — If the items are within 1 percent to 2 percent of the count, the system may be set to not record the adjustment. If large quantities of very inexpensive parts are being stored, it may be difficult and cost prohibitive to count out exact amounts when issuing and storing such items. However, accuracy may be improved by use of weight for the issuance of such items.

- Procurement policies — Economic Order Quantity (EOQ), lot size multiplier, minimum buys, level of spend and other similar policies are procurement policies put in place to assure the inventory items are purchased at the best possible cost/benefit. However, in the last few decades, price has been only one factor taken into consideration and may not be the overriding issue. Policies today are as likely to exist for quality and delivery timeliness as they do for price.

K) **Location of materials (for example, secure storeroom, outside yard storage, etc.)** — Physical location and the storage of materials are important. A few of the major considerations of how and where items are stored depends on the method of movement needed and each item's characteristics. The availability and location of facilities internationally will most certainly vary depending on the country. The organization may need to make long-term investment decisions to establish international storage facilities. If a decision is made to use existing international facilities, then the warehouse condition must be closely analyzed to ensure the products and storage containers will fit within the facility's parameters.

Any items that are considered at high risk for pilferage must be kept in a secure location. If the use of certain items is to be charged to a particular department, these items may require special security arrangements, as well.

Hazardous goods should be stored in an area that has special structures, such as flammable resistant cabinets or rooms with sprinkler systems. Some hazardous items cannot be stored together and must be separated by containment walls and ceilings. While mint would not normally be considered a hazardous material, the odor and flavor of mint will permeate all other materials in close proximity. For this reason, a maker of many flavors of tea may store its mint in a room separated from all other materials.

If movable trailers or containers are used for inventory storage, the inventory system should include location codes for trailer numbers, yard locations and other necessary information. A good inventory storage system will include location codes even if the inventory items are not required to be movable.

Satellite systems, coupled with RFID scanning and reading systems, have made possible the global tracking of inventory items as they are shipped almost anywhere in the world. Items can be tracked by the minute and scheduled receipts may be based on the known location of the goods. Containers coming from an international source can be off-loaded at a port and then transported to a 3PL warehouse. Sophisticated systems can record all these movements, and the buyer of the materials, or other persons with need to know, can track the location at any time. At any time during the shipment, the goods will be tracked to a location, vessel, port, rail car, highway trailer, third-party warehouse or other location with scanning and recording equipment.

L) **Master data management** — Organizations today often have multiple systems, such as logistics, CRM and ERP, each containing a different data set which is used by various business functions, processes and applications. These data sets vary in that they contain data that may differ, overlap, be incomplete or contain inaccuracies. As a result it is often difficult to get a true picture of customers, suppliers, products or inventory. To resolve this issue, organizations are adopting a master data management solution that will provide an accurate master repository which can be accessed by all areas of the organization.

BIBLIOGRAPHY

Bazerman, M.H. and M.D. Watkins. Predictable Surprises: *The Disasters You Should Have Seen Coming, and How to Prevent Them*, Harvard Business School Press, # 1764, 2004.

Burt, D.N., D.W Dobler and S. Starling. *World Class Supply Management: The Key to Supply Chain Management*, 7th edition, McGraw-Hill/Irwin, New York, 2002.

Cavinato, J.L., A.E. Flynn, M.L. Harding, C.S. Lallatin, M.L. Peck, H.M. Pohlig, S.R. Sturzl and V. Tucker (Eds.). ISM *Glossary of Key Supply Management Terms*, 6th edition, Institute for Supply Management®, Tempe, AZ, 2014.

Coyle, J.J., E.J. Bardi and C.J. Langley. *Management of Business Logistics: A Supply Chain Perspective*, 7th edition, South-Western College Publishing, Cincinnati, OH, 2002.

Czinkota, M.R., I.A. Ronkainen and M.H. Moffett. *International Business*, 8th edition, John Wiley & Sons, 2011.

Fisher, T. "Demystifying Master Data Management," CIO, April 30, 2007, http://www.cio.com/article/106811/Demystifying_Master_Data_Maagement.

Glover, B. and H. Bhatt. RFID Essentials, Theory in Practice [ILLUSTRATED], O'Reilly Media, Inc., 2006.

Harvard Business Essentials: Crisis Management: Master the Skills to Prevent Disasters. Harvard Business School Press, Product # 4376, 2004.

International Organization for Standardization. www.iso.org, "Supply chain security," June 2013.

Jacobs, F.R., W.L. Berry and D.C. Whybark. *Manufacturing Planning and Control Systems For Supply Chain Management: APICS/CPIM Certification Edition*, McGraw-Hill/Irwin, 2011.

Johnson, P.F., M. Leenders and A.E. Flynn. *Purchasing and Supply Management*, 13th edition, McGraw-Hill/Irwin, New York, 2005.

Monczka, R.M., R.J. Trent and R.B. Handfield. *Purchasing and Supply Chain Management*, 5th edition, South-Western CENGAGE Learning, 2011.

National Transportation Library. http://www.rita.dot.gov/, U.S. Department of Transportation, Research and Innovative and Technology Administration, May 2013.

Ross, D.F. *Distribution Planning and Control: Managing in the Era of Supply Chain Management,* 2nd edition, Springer, 2003.

Stanley, L. and D. Matthews. *Effective Supply Management Performance,* ISM Professional Series, Institute for Supply Management®, Tempe, AZ, 2014.

Violino, B. "RFID Business Applications," RFID Journal, January 16, 2005, http://www.rfidjournal.com/articles/view?1334/3.

Task 2-C-3

Coordinate and/or monitor the movement of equipment and assets within the organization.

1) Organizational policy for asset classification

The process of grouping economic resources under appropriate categories is asset classification. Asset categories would include current assets, fixed assets, intangible assets, investment assets and deferred costs. Assets are classified to facilitate the organization's financial health. These assets are defined as:

- Current assets — The short-term resources owned by a company, including cash, inventory and accounts receivable (ISM *Glossary* 2014). These assets have a life of one year or less or the normal operating cycle of the organization.

- Fixed assets — Defined as an asset that lasts more than a year, with an impact on shareholder value and considered by management to be worth controlling (ISM *Glossary* 2014). Fixed assets are usually referred to as property, plant and equipment. They are depreciated when they are over a certain monetary value. Depreciation is the recovery of a capital investment over time by expensing a portion in each financial period. Depreciation is a non-cash expense that reduces an organization's reported income. Amortization is a similar treatment for intangible asset use, costing and control.

- Intangible assets — These include assets such as a brand name, goodwill or reputation that have value but cannot be physically seen or touched (ISM *Glossary* 2014). Intangibles usually have a life in excess of one year. An example of an intangible asset is goodwill from having purchased another organization for an amount greater than the sum of its net worth.

- Investment assets — This is the use of capital to create more money, either through income producing vehicles or through risk-oriented ventures designed to result in capital gains.

- Deferred cost — This is the incurring of an expenditure that has a future benefit in excess of one year that is capitalized to an asset account.

These assets are usually classified by specific accounting rules established by the AICPA or the SEC in the United States. The organization's policies and procedures should be periodically reviewed to ensure they are consistent with these established rules as well as the reporting requirements established by the Sarbanes-Oxley Act. Internationally there are other organizations that specify the country's accounting rules. The International Financial Reporting Standards (IFRS) published by the International Accounting Standards Board are used by many companies around the world including those in the European Union.

Inventory policies are aligned with the term "current assets." The processes, policies and procedures for inventory control should be designed to meet the overall business objectives and to satisfy customers, internal or external. Organizations will typically use the inventory classification systems discussed in Task 2-C-2 such as first in-first out (FIFO), last in-first out (LIFO) or ABC inventory classification system.

Capital expenditure policies are more aligned with the term "fixed asset." These fixed assets have an impact on shareholder value and are considered by management worth controlling. Proposed assets are typically evaluated prior to purchase. The supply management professional will perform cost comparisons such as lease versus buy scenarios.

2) Tax policy on assets

Tax policies can vary from country to country. In the United States certain assets may qualify for the IRS Section 179 deduction for depreciation. This deduction allows organizations to deduct a portion of the total cost of the asset over its useful life. Ideally, the useful life of the asset is more than five years. Qualifying assets must be tangible, purchased for business use and on the IRS eligibility list. Some examples of qualifying assets include machinery, software and supplies. The IRS sets a maximum on the allowed dollar exemption each year depending on the type of business (for example, partnership, S Corporation, other type of corporation) and business income. Each year that the deduction for depreciation is taken reduces the asset's adjusted cost basis. More on this topic can be found at www.irs.gov/publications/p946/ch02.html#en_US_2012_publink1000107395.

3) Physical tracking systems (for example, bar coding, asset tags, serial numbers, Radio Frequency Identification — RFID)

Any asset that is considered of value to the organization and its stakeholders must be monitored and tracked. Assets can move from one department to another or even arrive in some other organization's inventory. The system each organization chooses to implement to track its asset will be predicated on the complexity, volume and/or frequency of use.

A popular way to track fixed assets is to implement asset tags. Asset tags provide a record of the asset and can verify ownership. Asset tagging is often accomplished through bar codes for easy and accurate information.

A bar code is a machine readable code — a pattern of alternating parallel bars and spaces, representing numbers and other characters. The major advantages of using bar coding technology in receiving and store operations include the reduction in error rate and improved entry speed and count accuracy. The bar codes provide an easy, precise and cost-effective method of identification by using a unique identification number (UID). The cost associated with asset management by bar coding is minimal and the benefits are plentiful.

Adding serial numbers to an asset tag will improve the tracking integrity. Serial numbers on asset tags also add value to the reliability of security. Serializing is a method of printed alpha and numerical characters arranged using an alpha/numerical sequence. The serial numbers can be based on a fixed asset department or on a master list. It is common to use special characters in the prefix to create a unique set of numbers for the identification of the type of asset, the department or for assets purchased in a particular year.

Radio frequency identification (RFID), as discussed in Task 2-C-2, is a passive or active radio data chip that is attached to products to allow retailers to track, access and compile data as part of the supply chain flow process (ISM *Glossary* 2014). RFID is the technology that is required for real-time physical tracking of equipment and assets. RFID monitors and tracks assets as they move and reports on status of the location. This technology will identify any deviations from the norm and report on those conditions. RFID validates and maintains the correct accurate physical inventories with less labor than if traditional bar coding methods were used. The RFID system may include alerts and triggers that report on any nonconforming procedures in the asset management policy.

Tracking assets is an important concern for every organization regardless of size. While employees may use a specific tool or a number of different tools, the asset ultimately belongs to the organization and must be returned. Therefore, without an accurate method for keeping track of these assets, it would be very easy for an organization to lose control of them.

Asset tracking software is available that will help any size business track valuable assets such as equipment, supplies and inventory.

Asset tracking software allows organizations to track what assets it owns, where each is located, who has it, when it was checked out, when it is due for return, when it is scheduled for maintenance, and the cost and depreciation of each asset. Many assets of organizations are on the property of customers and suppliers. Too many times the same organization might have assets on the property that are actually owned by a supplier, customer or another company or organization. Examples are tools, dies, packaging equipment, pallets, control- and quality-checking devices, computers, software and even leased items. Tracking systems are essential to keep track of such assets.

Other automated methods for tracking equipment and inventory include optical character reading (OCR), machine vision, magnetic stripe and surface acoustic wave (SAW).

Sarbanes-Oxley Act compliance policies have mandated publicly owned corporations to make significant changes in the methods that fixed assets are tracked and managed. Records and controls need to be documented, policies are imposed and need to be adhered to, physical asset inventories performed and audit trails sustained. (See Tasks 1-B-4 and 3-B-5 for more information on the Sarbanes-Oxley Act.)

4) Financial tracking systems

Tracking the value of an asset is required by all organizations. Measuring the net value and reporting the value are key performance indicators on how well an organization is performing financially. Accuracy of the data used for this process is critical. Communications and validating the equipment of the asset is essential to the success of financial reporting. Capital assets are typically assigned to a schedule in which their value is depreciated for a predetermined period of time.

A) **Capital equipment** — As defined in the ISM *Glossary* (2014), capital equipment is equipment used by an organization for its production potential that costs more than a predetermined threshold value and the cost of which will be depreciated over time. There are basic equipment and asset tracking systems like commercial spreadsheet programs. These can be a useful tool for setting up simple methods of tracking assets as they are purchased through their life cycle. Excel can be charted for analytical use and be simply graphed for visual presentation.

Also, most advanced fixed asset tracking software systems include implementing RFID or bar coding tracking devices to assure the asset is properly documented. These commercial software and hardware systems are readily available and most can be purchased as built-on tools for standard ERP systems. Modules inside the ERP system can be programmed and/or customized to manage the tracking of capital assets similar to the way inventory is tracked.

All these software and other financial tools can track capital equipment and should have methods of tracking the deprecation values of the assets in addition to the other requirements.

B) **Software tracking system** — There are many software programs available to track inventory and assets for organizations. Programs can be complex, such as an integrated tracking system, or as simple as a spreadsheet.

5) Internal distribution (for example, distribution channels)

Internal distribution is the moving of materials, such as raw materials, parts and sub-assemblies within the organization, whether to an internal customer or to the next stage of the manufacturing process.

A) **Internal transportation** — Internal transportation relates to the infrastructure in an organization that allows materials to be moved. Pallet jacks, forklifts, conveyer belts and storage-and-retrieval machines are examples of internal transportation equipment.

6) Types of equipment and assets (for example, vehicles, aircraft, railroad cars, copiers)

Equipment and assets vary from organization to organization. Cars, airlines, railroad cars, copiers, computers, machinery and finished goods are examples. These typically are items used in the production or delivery of goods or services to meet internal and external customer requirements.

7) Asset management

Asset management is the process of tracking fixed assets that an organization owns and has listed on its balance sheet. Most organizations track their assets using inventory management software, bar coding or RFID tools. After assigning a unique code to each asset, it is then scanned and the information is entered into a database.

The purpose of asset management and tracking of the asset is to sustain accurate financial accounts, to prevent theft and to manage the movement of the organization's assets.

An asset management program should have assigned responsibility of ownership. Particular attention should be paid to the financial reporting process for detail and accuracy. The process encompasses the purchase, use and disposal of assets with the aspiration to maximize the return on investment for each corporate asset. Assets should be used to their fullest potential; after their useful value has expired, the asset should be evaluated for disposal.

A) **Inventory management** — Inventory management is defined as the business function concerned with planning and controlling inventory (ISM *Glossary* 2014). However, an inventory of fixed assets is different than an inventory of expendable goods that are managed in a manufacturing process. The latter represents raw materials, components and finished goods that are expended and replenished on an ongoing basis and normally have experienced staff focused on inventory control. Developing and implementing an inventory management system is discussed in Task 2-C-2.

For most of the other types of organizational assets, usually IT and finance are the primary stakeholders in managing the asset tracking unless the organization has a dedicated asset or facility management department. In either case the tracking methods are similar.

Many department managers do not normally keep track of what they are replacing or removing. IT and/or finance usually are accountable for collecting, reporting and performing physical inventories of the organization's assets.

There are numerous tools and software programs available commercially. Most of these packages include a serialized bar coding tool that allows the detailed tracking of the assets. Human resources (HR) plays a key role in this process.

If someone is hired or leaves the organization, HR usually is responsible for asking what equipment the employee needs or had, and where is it located.

Usually IT, finance and HR work as one entity and are accountable for acquisition, collecting data on location, reporting and performing physical inventories of the organization's assets along with reporting the financial obligations of asset value for government reporting requirements.

B) **Asset recovery** — Assets should be used to their fullest potential and be maintained properly during their life cycle. After the asset has exceeded it usefulness, the practice of asset recovery begins.

Asset recovery is the re-employment, reuse, recycling or regeneration of something of value (property, equipment, goods and so on) that is no longer necessary for the original intent, or the return of environmental conditions to the state they were prior to an action (ISM *Glossary* 2014). Finding a new use for existing assets is a good business practice. It can minimize environmental impacts and reduce an organization's disposal costs. In some cases, the asset or the entire organization may be in the process of going through asset retirement, bankruptcy or foreclosure.

Assets represent a significant investment for any organization. They must be classified, tracked and monitored during their life cycle, and when appropriate, must be disposed of in a manner that results in maximum return.

During the asset recovery process, the organization will have an outsourced expert, an asset recovery organization, or a staff employee who specializes in this area. Determining the potential value of the assets as residual value is complicated due to the financial risks that are associated with the decisions. If the decision is to outsource the services to an asset recovery organization, that organization will manage the entire process.

The objective of asset recovery is to increase the cash position of the organization by optimizing the return on the assets.

Through the process of asset recovery, some of the action items consist of the following:

- Identifying for removal the asset from the organization's asset inventory

- Consideration for asset tracking and inventory accuracy

- Data security and removal of organization information

- Environmental compliance, current and cradle-to-grave or cradle-to-cradle responsibilities (see Task 3-B-7 for more information)

- Logistics, storage and handling

- Life-cycle completions

- Value analysis and optimal return from the asset.

All issues in these areas must be addressed and resolved before removing the asset from the organization's balance sheet.

C) **Equipment lending** — Equipment may be loaned to others for a variety of reasons. Some of the primary reasons include:

- An organization can determine if the equipment will function as required before purchase or lease

- A business relationship can be facilitated

- A disaster has occurred and one organization lends another organization equipment to assist it with returning to full operating capacity.

D) **Asset disposal** — Disposing of assets no longer useful is the last step in the supply management process. When an asset has exceeded its usefulness and cannot be recycled, remanufactured, re-employed or reused, or an organization has surplus, disposal takes place. Supply management professionals should determine the options available to maximize disposal value and reduce risk and liability to the organization within the bounds of all applicable laws and regulations. Internet/intranet and e-auctions are commonly used to sell surplus assets. Third-party brokers or sellers can also be used. Obsolete items can be donated to charity and may have a tax deduction benefit. Approval for disposal may be needed depending on the value of the asset.

BIBLIOGRAPHY

Cavinato, J.L., A.E. Flynn and R.G. Kauffman (Eds.). *The Supply Management Handbook*, 7th edition, McGraw-Hill, New York, 2006.

Cavinato, J.L., A.E. Flynn, M.L. Harding, C.S. Lallatin, M.L. Peck, H.M. Pohlig, S.R. Sturzl and V. Tucker (Eds.). ISM *Glossary of Key Supply Management Terms*, 6th edition, Institute for Supply Management®, Tempe, AZ, 2014.

Nolan, L.D. "Cash in on Unproductive Assets," *Purchasing Today*, July 1996, p. 6.

InvestorWords, www.investorwords.com, July 27, 2007.

Piasecki, D.J. *Inventory Accuracy, People, Processes and Technology*, OPS Publishing, Kenosha, WI, 2003.

Stanley, L. and D. Matthews. *Effective Supply Management Performance*, ISM Professional Series, Institute for Supply Management®, Tempe, AZ, 2014.

Norris, F. "The Case for Global Accounting," *New York Times*, May 10, 2012, www.nytimes.com, May 2, 2013.

Wade, D.S. "Investment Recovery Strategies," *Inside Supply Management*®, July 2007, p. 30.

Waters, D. *Inventory Control and Management*, 2nd edition, John Wiley & Sons Ltd., England, 2003.

TASK 2-C-4
Develop, oversee and execute multichannel disposition plan for excess inventory and finished goods.

1) Investment recovery principles

The ISM *Glossary* (2014) defines investment recovery as a systematic, centralized organizational effort to manage the surplus or obsolete equipment, material and scrap recovery/marketing/disposition activities in a manner that recovers as much of the original capital investment as possible. Investment recovery principles are the means of developing procedures and systems that manage the ownership cost over the complete life cycle of the acquired inventory investment. The value of this inventory is an important consideration — as much as the acquisition cost of the inventory. Life-cycle management conceptually is the planning method to ensure that the most cost-effective tactical approach for the product is being achieved.

Developing and managing investment recovery is a complex matter. Models are developed to manage the inventories that can be re-engineered to increase or revise the current state to add value to the business goals, and/or to convert the asset to cash by reselling or disposing of the asset.

It is important to understand and correctly value the inventory to be able to price the goods, whether they are being sent back to the supplier, sold on the open market, donated or even scrapped.

A) **Value stream mapping** — Value stream mapping originally was a lean manufacturing technique in which the transformation of materials is traced from beginning to end to determine if there is waste in the process either in the form of a step where no value is added or a point of "wait time" when material is being stored to await further value-adding transformation. This concept may also be applied to services (ISM *Glossary* 2014).

One technique used in value stream mapping is the flow process chart, which is used to identify the value-add content in the process documentation stage of the analysis. The flow process chart is a simple half-text, half-picture method of showing the steps in a process, using symbols to indicate the type of action being taken and text to give details of the action. The chart can be used to show what happens to selected people, materials or equipment.

Process mapping is a method of drawing a pictorial representation of a process (for example, manufacturing a component or ordering a part) that breaks the process into key activities, transfers, decisions and approvals. Process maps enable analysis of the inputs, outputs and interrelationships of each process to understand how processes interact in a system, locate process flaws that are creating systemic problems, evaluate which activities add value for the customer, mobilize teams to streamline and improve processes, and identify processes that need to be re-engineered. Other commonly used terms are flow charting, flow diagrams, process diagrams and workflow diagrams (ISM *Glossary* 2014).

This is an example of a process map on warehousing cost analysis:

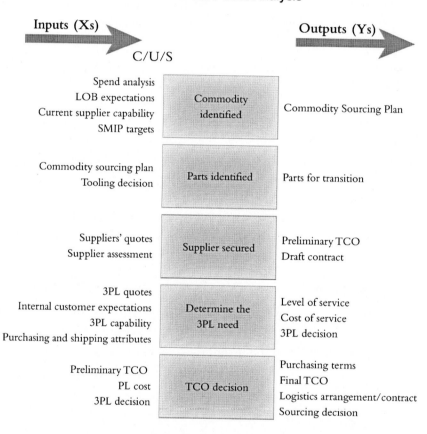

3PL Warehouse Cost Analysis

Source: Vivek Nair, Six Sigma Black Belt, Cummins Power Generation.

B) **Security of disposal** — Ownership must be documented during disposal of excess inventory, whether the business is returning it to the supplier of origin, selling it on the open market or disposing of the goods as scrap. Original equipment manufacturer (OEM) businesses are becoming more accountable for their products' disposal.

Numerous governing agencies are setting international standards in the disposal and security of disposing hazardous materials. (See Task 3-B-7 regarding the managing and disposing of hazardous materials.)

A few of the regulations dealing with controlling the levels of security include the following:

- OSHA and EPA are commonly known agencies in the United States that have strict rules overseeing the security of disposed products and byproducts.

- RoHS and WEEE are acronyms for the European Union rules for controlling hazardous materials (described below).

- RoHS (The Restriction of Hazardous Substances Directive) affects many electronic components that use lead-based solder, and are being replaced by lead-free components. This is causing engineering to do research to verify that the lead-free offering matches specifications with the leaded version. Engineering Change Notices and new "Item Masters" are then required to change the supplier part numbers of what is purchased.

- The WEEE (Waste Electrical and Electronic Equipment) rules apply to goods sold in the free market. The rules strive to prevent these products from going to a landfill. The policies are, in particular, to preserve, protect and improve the quality of the environment, protect human health and use natural resources.

RoHS was adopted in February 2003 by the European Union and took effect on July 1, 2006. This directive restricted the use of six hazardous materials in the manufacture of various types of electronic and electrical equipment, including:

1) Lead

2) Mercury

3) Cadmium

4) Chromium VI (also known as hexavalent chromium or Cr6+)

5) PBB

6) PBDE.

PBB and PBDE are flame retardants used in some plastics.

The following are the 10 official categories of WEEE and RoHS products. The WEEE regulations apply to all categories. The RoHS regulations apply to categories 1, 2, 3, 4, 5, 6, 7 and 10:

1) Large household appliances

2) Small household appliances

3) IT and telecommunications equipment

4) Consumer equipment

5) Lighting equipment

6) Electrical and electronic tools (with the exception of large-scale stationary industrial tools)

7) Toys, leisure and sports equipment

8) Medical devices (with the exception of all implanted and infected products)

9) Monitoring and control instruments

10) Automatic dispensers.

In 2008 the European Union amended the original directive, now known as RoHS2 (RoHS Directive 2011/65/EU), which became law in July 2011. The new law will be phased in over eight years. RoHS2 extends its restrictions to all electronic equipment, cables and spare parts. However, there are also a number of exclusions, including military equipment, equipment meant to go into space, large-scale stationary industrial tools, large-scale fixed installations, means of transport, non-road mobile machinery for professional use, active implantable medical devices, photovoltaic panels and R&D equipment made available only on a business-to-business basis. Lastly, manufacturers, distributors and importers will have to meet certain legal requirements for marking products for identification and tracing, demonstrating compliance with set standards and keeping technical documentation for 10 years.

California modeled its 2007 law in line with Europe's RoHS and some countries, such as Norway, Switzerland and China have enacted similar legislation.

The primary objective of these types of agencies is to hold responsibility over the individual or business when manufacturing and disposing of the product. This, in turn, makes the security of disposal critical and organizations must maintain records of ownership of the products they are producing during the cradle-to-grave life cycle. The responsibilities do not end at the disposal process for the producing organization. The originating business is ultimately accountable for any and all issues that may surface due to environmental policies.

Controlling the security of the product during the entire stage of the manufacturing process through life cycle completion is important. Documentation and transfer of ownership records must be maintained to assure accountability for the proper handling of the goods.

2) Marketplace for disposal

After inventory is classified as obsolete or excessive and the effective decision made to dispose of the goods, a number of options are available. The most cost-effective way to dispose of inventory is to sell it back to the supplier. This process is sometimes called buy-back. If the supplier has another customer using the item, it will be an attractive option for them. The current supplier may charge a restocking fee of a certain percentage and then sell it for full value to another customer.

A) **Broker** — Many organizations will contract with a brokerage organization that specializes in reselling goods on behalf of the seller. The ISM *Glossary* defines a broker as an intermediary who, for a fee, brings a buyer and seller together. A broker may also provide additional services to the purchaser. The broker has no ownership of the goods being sold. Payment and credit transactions remain the responsibility of the buyer and seller. The broker does not take possession of the goods being sold. This is more common in the spare parts and aftermarket sale of goods. An example of this would be an organization that must dispose of excessive quantities of spare parts motors no longer needed for maintenance issues. There may be a future requirement for the item but the demand has fallen off drastically. The organization may authorize a broker to sell a certain amount of the inventory at a target price.

B) **Dealer** — A dealer is similar to a broker except it usually will take possession of the goods and sell them. The dealer fee for services is typically a commission calculated on the total value of the sale.

C) **Third-party specialist** — In some cases, a global organization may contract with a service organization to handle the spare parts business of the organization. This business can be considered a profit center or a cost center, based on whether it is a stand-alone entity. Depending how the contract is written, the service organization may be able to sell to the open market and be classified as a profit center and operate independent from the parent organization. It could also be a cost center and operate under the direction of the parent organization.

If the organization works independently, it will be responsible for its own profit/loss statement, inventory assets and operating costs, and will not have to report back to the parent organization.

3) Categories

A) **Surplus** — Surplus or excessive inventory is any inventory that is greater than current or future planned demand. There is usually a period of time that consists of a review period for the demand. It can include inventory items as well as non-inventory assets that may fall under the control of supply management.

In some manufacturing sites, demand period is a period of time in the future plus the usage during a period of time in the past. An example would be looking at all demand for any item in the last 12 months and looking at the forecast demand for the next 12 months. If there is demand for the item quantity of 100 units but the on-hand inventory is 175 units, then 75 units will be surplus or excessive.

Surplus inventory is sometimes caused by the need to order in lot sizes that are not matched to consumption lot sizes. If a supplier requires the item to be purchased in lots of 100 but the manufacturing lot size is different from the 100 units, mismatched inventory quantities will be created.

Methods to control this are difficult and risky. Supply management could purchase less than lot size but most likely will have to accept an unfavorable purchase price variance.

B) **Obsolete** — Inventory of any kind is considered obsolete if there no longer is demand for the item. Goods that require use before a certain date or period of time and are not consumed by that time are classified as having expired shelf life and no longer are acceptable to be used or sold.

In manufacturing, bill of material (BOM) revisions are daily occurrences in developing process improvement incentives. When revisions are executed, the options are to phase out and consume the item, or immediately dispose of the part.

Sometimes the component is in upper or lower levels of the BOM and will not be completely consumed before the remaining items are consumed. This causes the balance of these parts to be obsolete and have no value.

The incentive would be to sell back to the supplier, salvage for scrap value or scrap and write off the inventory asset.

C) **Damaged** — Damaged material goods are no longer fit for use. Often rework or repair is impractical. This damage can occur due to defective manufacturing, improper handling or inadequate packaging. An inventory adjustment is completed to classify the item as non-nettable so the planning department will not consider it available to satisfy a demand requirement.

Goods that are damaged are identified and classified as nonconforming materials and require deposition through rework or scrap. If the goods can be reworked to a state equal to or greater than the original state, they can then be transferred back into a nettable state and be used. The reworked item must be the same fit, form and function specified for the original item.

BIBLIOGRAPHY

Cavinato, J.L., A.E. Flynn and R.G. Kauffman (Eds.). *The Supply Management Handbook*, 7th edition, McGraw-Hill, New York, 2006.

Cavinato, J.L., A.E. Flynn, M.L. Harding, C.S. Lallatin, M.L. Peck, H.M. Pohlig, S.R. Sturzl and V. Tucker (Eds.). ISM *Glossary of Key Supply Management Terms*, 6th edition, Institute for Supply Management®, Tempe, AZ, 2014.

European Commission, "Recast of the RoHS Directive," http://ec.europa.eu/environment/waste/rohs_eee/index_en.htm, accessed June 23, 2013.

Stanley, L. and D. Matthews. *Effective Supply Management Performance*, ISM *Professional Series*, Institute for Supply Management®, Tempe, AZ, 2014.

Organization/Department Assessment

Task 2-D-1

Monitor work against business plans and take action to resolve variances or adjust plans as appropriate.

One of the major functions of management is to evaluate and control the performance of an activity. A supply management organization is certainly no exception. An organization's leadership team must be able to evaluate overall performance of its organization, departments, individuals and suppliers. Creating meaningful measurements, collecting data and communicating the results are a key role of management. This can be difficult, because there is no one set or collection of metrics that works for all supply management organizations. It is the responsibility of management to create, report, achieve, evaluate and revise the organizational metrics that will assist it in improving its strategic position within the larger organization to meet its corporate objectives.

1) Performance measurement processes

Performance measurement processes are intended to enable clear communication of goals, and focus effort and resources around key business objectives. These processes allow clear measurement of results against expectations. They should also be reviewed frequently to ensure desired behavior is being reinforced so appropriate actions can be taken to resolve variances as necessary.

A) **What to measure** — What is measured is determined by the overall business objectives of the organization. These measurements should reinforce the activities and processes to attain these objectives.

Measurements can be broken down into broad categories of performance metrics: financial, operational, information technology, sourcing, business control and relationship.

- Examples of financial metrics include:

  — Cost reductions reflect an effort to lower costs associated with acquiring a particular product or service (ISM *Glossary* 2014). They demonstrate the value-add of the supply management team when purchasing goods or services.

  — Year-to-year cost reductions

  — Supply management competitive advantage comes from cost reduction measurements that measure (using market intelligence) how well a team is buying versus the competition's organization.

— Productivity metrics measure total cost of supply management labor versus total organization revenue.

— Supply management efficiency measures total cost savings to supply management labor expense.

— Average payment terms.

- Examples of operational metrics:

    — Supplier assurance — delivery

    — Supplier quality metrics — Field impacts, shipped products quality level, warranty expense

    — Contracted labor utilization rates.

- Examples of information technology metrics:

    — Supplier transaction index measures how well the suppliers are connected to the buying organization from an electronic invoicing/purchase order generation, etc. point of view.

    — Total e-spend measures the percentage of spend that is paid via electronic payment.

- Examples of sourcing metrics:

    — Leverage spending determines the number of the organization's suppliers that makes up 80 percent of the total spend (the 80/20 rule).

    — Diversity supplier spending measures total spend with diversity suppliers.

    — Direct and indirect spend addressed

    — New product development participation.

- Examples of business control and relationship metrics:

    — Internal and external client satisfaction surveys of supply management

    — Supplier surveys

    — Supplier report cards survey internal clients regarding their satisfaction with suppliers.

B) **Measurement creation** — Measurements/metrics must begin with a view of meeting and exceeding the organization's key strategies and mission statements. Using this as the baseline, a clear and concise endpoint can be developed for the creation of these measurements.

Supply management objectives must be aligned, and work in conjunction, with those of the rest of the organization. The integration of objectives ensures success of the vision, mission and goals of the organization. It is imperative that the supply management organization understands its relationship with those in the larger organization.

Not all objectives should receive the same priority, so it is necessary to first pursue those that have the greatest impact on the operation of the organization. These priorities should be established and communicated throughout the organization to ensure the objectives and the assigned priorities are valid.

Measurements and personal objectives for the organization must flow downward. The senior executive within an organization must start with a set of metrics, which then flows down throughout the rest of the organization.

C) **Results evaluation (signal versus noise, key stakeholders)** — Objectives need to be divided into groups (for example, cost savings and product improvement) that can be quantified and measured. Quantifying the existing situation, and then comparing the situation at some point in the future against historical data or against appropriate external benchmarks, is one way to do this. The key to effective measurement is the selection of elements to measure that focus attention and resources on how and when supply management can add the maximum value to the organization.

D) **Key Performance Indicators (KPIs)** — KPIs are measurements considered critical to the performance of a business or process, usually calculated and reviewed on a regular basis (ISM *Glossary* 2014). KPIs are quantifiable measurements, agreed to beforehand, that reflect the critical success factors of an organization. They differ depending on the organization.

One approach would be to meet with and review the key metrics of departments that the supply management department supports and then create key performance indicators that will measure results that will meet the goals of the department's key customers. Fundamentally, one of the objectives of supply management is the acquisition of materials and services of the right quality, in the right quantity, at the right price, at the right time and from the right source.

E) **Performance management systems (for example, earned value management system [EVMS], balanced scorecard, value stream)** — There are many approaches to managing performance. The key is that the way performance will be managed should result in buy-in or employee accountability throughout the entire organization. This can be accomplished by developing goals and objectives at the top of the organization and then sharing them downward while ensuring that each individual takes ownership of those metrics. This can be accomplished by including these metrics in the individual's personal performance criteria.

One metric is the earned value management system (EVMS), which is a management system and related sub-systems implemented to establish a relationship between cost, schedule and technical aspects of a project; measure progress; accumulate actual costs; analyze deviations from plans; forecast completion of events and incorporate changes in a timely manner (ISM *Glossary* 2014).

Another metric is value stream mapping, which is a lean manufacturing technique in which the transformation of materials is traced from beginning to end to determine if there is waste in the process. Such waste could be in the form of a step where no value is added or a point of "wait time" when material is being stored to await further value-adding transformation. This concept may also be applied to services (ISM *Glossary* 2014).

Scorecard systems for management awareness are one way of monitoring performance. This can be accomplished by setting up a monthly or quarterly review of the key metrics for the organization and then monitoring them based on results. For example, an organization might set a scale for each metric; if the metric is on track it is in a green light position and no review is needed. If it is in moderately good shape it is classified as a yellow light and it might be reviewed by a middle manager. If it is in bad shape, it is classified as a red light, is reviewed by senior management and a corrective action plan is required.

F) **Corrective action processes** — Corrective action is taken to bring a process that has veered off the planned course back on track (ISM *Glossary* 2014). When performance fails, it is appropriate to set up corrective action plans. This can be done at all levels of the organization and will depend on the degree of performance failure as to how high a level of management is involved. The process of determining a corrective action requires identification of actions that can be taken to prevent or mitigate the weakness. These are commonly referred to as countermeasures. Effectiveness is generally thought to be improved by addressing the root cause(s) of the problem.

These corrective action plans must be reviewed within the organization as well as with the suppliers. If correction is needed from the supplier, a formalized process should be implemented with the supplier to again meet the minimum level of performance expectations. These plans should include a time line for meeting the goals and penalties for not meeting them.

BIBLIOGRAPHY

Cavinato, J.L., A.E. Flynn, M.L. Harding, C.S. Lallatin, M.L. Peck, H.M. Pohlig, S.R. Sturzl and V. Tucker (Eds.). ISM *Glossary of Key Supply Management Terms*, 6th edition, Institute for Supply Management®, Tempe, AZ, 2014.

Mosconi, T. and P. Carter. *Strategic Measures and Measurement Systems for Purchasing and Supply*, presentation at ISM's 89th Annual International Supply Management Conference, April 2004.

Task 2-D-2
Develop performance criteria and evaluate supply management staff performance.

A major function of management is to clearly establish business objectives for the organization and to evaluate the performance of supply management professionals at all levels. Some of the good practices used in supply management performance and measurement state that the measures must be:

- Aligned vertically and horizontally — Measures are aligned with key corporate objectives, individual performance objectives, strategic objectives of business units and strategic objectives of functional groups.

- Comprehensive — Measures cover all areas where supply management can impact marketplace success.

- Dynamic and aggressive — Measures are adjusted regularly for changes in priorities and represent a challenge to the organization, although the goals are achievable.

- Transparent and broadly communicated — Measures are clearly and broadly communicated to ensure they are used to drive decision-making.

- Tied to incentive compensation — Measures are tied to meaningful performance-based incentives.

- Backed with resources — Measures are supported by resources to set meaningful targets and to measure performance.

- Championed by strong leadership — Supply management is committed to a performance measurement process that identifies the right measures and targets. The measurement process meets the targets and is used to set budgets, plans and resource allocation. It brings savings to the bottom line or it is reinvested appropriately (Mosconi and Carter 2004).

1) Issues in the evaluation of employees

When evaluating employees, care must be taken to objectively measure their contributions to the organization's goals. In addition to quantitative measures, subjective factors such as employee behaviors can also be taken into consideration for an overall evaluation.

A) **Align employee objectives to organizational goals** — The supply management department's goals should be developed at the most senior executive levels to ensure they are consistent with the overall business model and the strategic direction of the organization. These goals are then cascaded through the organization so each supply management professional can develop personal business objectives. It is the supply management professional's responsibility to ensure that each employee objective supports the organizational goals.

B) **Determine success criteria** — The criteria for success are a direct result of the organization's mission, strategies and objectives. Supply management departments must identify how they can contribute to the organization's objectives, and then develop measurements that will move the function in a direction that will reinforce those objectives. For example, if the organization's objective is to be the low-cost producer, the supply management department criterion will be to find low-cost suppliers without negatively impacting other organizational objectives, such as quality and delivery.

C) **Determine appraisal factors** — There are many factors which go into the appraisal/assessment of employees. A starting point would be the essential functions of the job. Given the significant responsibilities and impact to business, quantitative as well as qualitative factors should be considered when assessing the contribution of supply management professionals.

　　1.0　**Quantitative** — Quantitative factors are those performance elements that can be measured numerically, such as cost, quality and delivery performance.

　　2.0　**Qualitative** — Qualitative factors are those performance elements that are more subjective to measure, such as teamwork, creativity, responsiveness to change and customer focus. When considering these factors, care should be taken to apply solid judgment in the overall assessment.

D) **Sources of feedback** — Input from multiple sources on employee contributions is an important element of properly assessing their contributions to the organization. Valuable input can be gained by direct interaction with others and their review of the supply management professional's results. Since the perception of the employee's contribution and behavior can be different among managers, peers, clients and suppliers, seeking input from multiple sources can allow for a more effective assessment.

　　1.0　**Team and/or peer** — Team and/or peer input are often the most valuable as this group has daily interaction with each other. They experience daily the contributions from their peers and knowledge of how they handle the ongoing challenges and opportunities.

2.0 **Self-assessment** — Self-assessments can be done by the supply management professional or as an organization. Periodic reviews of processes and results can also provide valuable input.

3.0 **Internal customer** — Internal customer input allows the supply management professional to assess how responsive the employee is to the client's needs and how clearly the requirements are understood.

4.0 **Supplier input** — Supplier input, through periodic surveys or direct input, provides still another perspective of the employee's effectiveness. The buyer/seller relationship can be complex so input from a supplier can provide valuable information.

5.0 **Interviews** — One of the most critical processes of evaluating supply management professionals is to provide effective feed-back to employees. Clear feedback to employees as to how effective they have achieved their personal business objectives should be provided. In addition, it is important that the supply management professional provide input to the employee on how they can improve their overall contribution to the organization. Equally important is for the employee to listen openly to sug-gested improvements so that continued improvements can be made by the employee and subsequently by the organization.

As part of this process, effective two-way communication is vital. Clear, open and honest dialogue in a nonconfrontational and nondefensive manner is essential.

6.0 **Customer input** — More supply management departments today are seeking feedback from their internal customers on their performance. This is frequently done through the use of online surveys, focus groups and one-on-one interviews (depending on size of organization and resources available). To improve the feedback process, supply management professionals should be involved in writing the questions for their customers (since they have frequent contact with the business units), deciding how the questions will be administered and determining the metrics that will be used. Questions should be posed in customer terms to obtain the best responses. Input should be requested on an annual basis at a time that is most convenient for the customer. Once the responses have been analyzed, it is important to share what has been learned with the customer and what steps will be taken to make improvements.

E) **Employee accountability (for example, performance improvement plan)** — As part of the performance assessment process, employees should understand how they can improve their overall contributions to the business. In the case of low performing employees, a clearly documented improvement plan that defines specific areas, metrics and dates should be established. This plan should also clearly state the consequences of not achieving and sustaining improved performance.

BIBLIOGRAPHY

Adapted from the C.P.M. *Study Guide*, 7th edition, Institute for Supply Management®, Tempe, AZ, 2001.

Mosconi, T. and P. Carter. *Strategic Measures and Measurement Systems for Purchasing and Supply*, presentation at ISM's 89th Annual International Supply Management Conference, April 2004.

Siegfried, M. "Building Relationships... Measuring Satisfaction." *Inside Supply Management®*, August 2012, p. 18.

Task 2-D-3
Develop tools and processes to measure, report and improve compliance with supply management policies.

One of the requirements of a supply management organization is to have available or develop tools/processes that can properly measure, report and improve compliance. While initially creating these tools/processes can seem laborious, they will be a key building block to creating a supply chain that can operate effectively on a global basis. When seamless processes and tools are created that can work throughout a supply chain without regard to country or region, the supply chain is managed efficiently and in compliance with the organization's policies.

1) **Audit processes** — The scope of an audit includes a wide range of activities, ranging from the maintenance of records through compliance with policy to the evaluation of functional and process efficiency and effectiveness.

   A systematic process for auditing global processes should be established. This can be done through internal audits or external audits. Most large organizations establish a system of regularly scheduled peer audits or reviews and are then followed up by audits performed by internal audit organizations within the corporation. Many of these audits are announced with very little time for preparation by the audited organization so they can't "change" anything in advance of the audit.

   A supply management audit is a comprehensive, systematic, independent and periodic examination of an organization's supply management environment, objectives, strategies and activities. It is used to identify strengths and weaknesses and to develop a plan to improve performance. Often, audits are conducted by outside consultants to ensure the necessary objectivity and independence of judgment. They are, however, also conducted internally.

   If an organization is found to be noncompliant with established procedures, a management review and process improvement plan will most likely be necessary. Depending on the severity of the audit findings, possible disciplinary action may be necessary.

2) **Validation process** — Validation implies the supply management professional is able to substantiate that a solution or process is correct or compliant with the set standards or rules. Validation usually relates to meeting the needs of an external or internal customer, or user of a product, service or system. The validation processes are established to ensure that the standards and rules are appropriate and comply with legal and regulatory requirements.

These process reviews can be accomplished internally or externally through outsourcing.

3) **Reporting requirements** — Every organization will have to establish a management reporting system or structure that will ensure measurements and processes are tracked on a regular basis for compliance and information accuracy issues. This can be done through established management meetings, audit meetings and peer review meetings.

4) **Remediation** — If a process deficiency is found through established audits or reviews, a process improvement plan should be established to correct the defect, establish solutions and define actions to be taken. Often a written action plan is necessary that includes a monitoring plan. Typically these action plans are due back to the auditor or reviewer.

5) **Training** — Supply management training and education should be ongoing, as the supply chain is continually evolving. Training on supply management policies and procedures to ensure compliance should obviously extend beyond supply management professionals. Supply management's customers must be kept informed of new procedures and policies. Organizations must establish a system of continuous improvement for their personnel. This can be done through Web-based education, face-to-face classes, lessons learned sharing and discussions after audit reviews. Most of this education or training can be accomplished internally by an organization or through external education sources.

6) **Compliance metrics** — Compliance metrics for any established process, procedure or policy should be quantifiable to gauge the organization's success. The primary metric is the level of adoption over a designated period of time. To achieve this compliance metric, a defined implementation process is established. The implementation process could include executive sponsorship, collaborative teams, use of change management techniques such as a communication plan and reporting requirements, and perhaps automated tracking and management.

   A) **Organizational policies (for example, supplier diversity, social responsibility)** — A policy is a plan to guide decisions and achieve rational outcomes. Policies are dynamic and for the most part can be changed relatively easily. Policies are typically disseminated through official written documents. Due to the nature of organizations today, corporate policies are established to guide the behaviors in the organization. However, regulatory policies, or mandates, limit the discretion of individuals and agencies, or otherwise compel certain types of behavior.

   Supplier diversity and social responsibility policies also must be observed.

- Supplier diversity policies — Many organizations establish policies with regard to purchasing from a diverse supply base. In the United States and in some other countries, government has supported special interest segments of society. Some governmental programs stipulate requirements for purchasing from a diverse supply base. Some organizations have recognized a growth in diverse markets and believe it is sound business practice to purchase from those diverse markets. The diverse supplier may include certified minority-owned business enterprises (MBE); women-owned business enterprises (WBE); business enterprises with gay, lesbian, bisexual or transgender (GLBT) ownership; and business enterprises owned by people with disabilities (PWD). For additional information on supplier diversity see Tasks 1-D-1, 1-E-2 and 1-F-3.

- Social responsibility policies — As organizations develop internationally to provide or obtain products and services, it is difficult and complex to be socially responsible. There is a variety of stakeholders, customs, business norms, practices, legal systems and ethical practices to balance. However, most organizations do establish policies and practices in terms of how they will buy, where they will buy and from whom they will buy. Many industries have developed standards regarding the suppliers with whom they will do business. These suppliers must comply with socially acceptable standards (child labor, sweatshops). For additional information on social responsibility see Task 1-D-1.

- Ethical supply management policies — Most organizations have established ethical policies and practices in the form of how business should be conducted by their employees. Many organizations have used ISM's *Principles and Standards of Ethical Supply Management Conduct* as their guide. See Task 1-D-1 for more information.

BIBLIOGRAPHY

Adapted from the C.P.M. *Study Guide*, 7th edition, Institute for Supply Management™, Tempe, AZ, 2001.

Hausmann, K. *Beyond Sourcing: How to Drive Additional Total Savings Year After Year*, presentation at ISM's 90th Annual International Supply Management Conference, San Antonio, TX, May 2005.

Johnson, P.F., M.R. Leenders and A.E. Flynn. *Purchasing and Supply Management*, 14th edition, McGraw-Hill/Irwin, New York, 2010.

Task 2-D-4

Analyze and resolve issues raised in supply management audit reports.

How well is the supply management department really doing? How well are its processes really working? Is the organization consistently following procedures? How do you know? The answers to these questions are normally acquired through an audit, in which objective evidence is gathered. An audit is more than a compilation of opinions. It is a structured process to determine whether an organization, process or product meets an agreed-upon standard. Reasons for undergoing an audit include:

- Prevention of mistakes and problems

- Gauging system and process efficiency and effectiveness. How do the policies work in practice? Repetitive or contradictory practices are easily identified through an audit. The supply management process may meet every organization policy, rule and procedure, and still may be seriously flawed.

- A regulatory or industry compliance requirement.

An audit usually gauges compliance with a given standard. Without a standard, a review exercise is not considered auditing, but rather it is simply investigating. Sample standards could include organizational policies, organizational procedures, contract requirements, regulatory requirements and ISO requirements.

1) Types of audits

A) **Internal** — One type of internal audit is self-inspection, which is the process of using an auditor who has a vested interest in the audit — hence the term "inspection" rather than "audit." A supply management department can be audited by individuals from that department. Self-inspection can be a valuable tool; however, it can be more easily biased.

A second type is an audit conducted by auditors who are employed by the organization being audited, but who have no vested interest in the audit results of the area being audited. If a supply management department is being audited, it may be audited by a team from another department. Advantages of an internal audit include ease of scheduling, flexibility and that the auditors already have an understanding of the organization. Disadvantages include difficulty in finding qualified auditors with technical or audit expertise; as well, the audit report may not be taken seriously, depending on the reputation of the auditors. The audit report may be submitted to designated management, the board of directors, or both.

Organizations abide by GAAP (Generally Accepted Accounting Principles), a widely accepted set of rules, conventions, standards and procedures for reporting financial information, as established by the U.S. Financial Accounting Standards Board (FASB) when conducting internal audits (ISM *Glossary* 2014). The International Financial Report Standards (IFRS) is another set of standards and interpretations adopted by the International Accounting Standards Board (IASB).

B) **External** — This type of audit is performed when an organization hires an outside auditor to audit the organization. An external auditor will probably conduct a preliminary interview to determine the audit scope and probably request a current organization chart, copies of procedures and any special requirements. Depending on the scope of the audit, it is common for the auditor to request a list of key suppliers or internal customers. Advantages of external audits are that the auditors are trained in the function, the audit report is more likely to be taken seriously, and the auditor has no vested interest in the outcome. A disadvantage is the cost and time to educate the auditors about the organization.

External audits in the United States must be in compliance with the Sarbanes-Oxley Act of 2002, a U.S. federal law commonly called SOX. This law was passed in an attempt to restore public confidence in corporate governance. It regulates the accounting profession and imposes extensive reporting requirements on all publicly traded corporations in the United States. The law requires internal financial controls to provide assurance of the reliability of financial reporting and preparation of financial statements (ISM *Glossary* 2014). There is some pressure on countries for the international harmonization of accounting standards. The European Union adopted the International Financial Reporting Standards (IFRS) in 2005.

2) Validation of current policies, procedures, work instructions and forms

The purpose of an audit could be as narrow as verifying that complete purchase orders are filed correctly, or as broad as an ISO 9000 systems audit. The purpose of the audit will also determine the resources required for the audit. Some other possible purposes include:

- Are proper monetary limits being adhered to?

- Are the appropriate personnel conducting transactions?

- Are suppliers' references and performance records being checked?

- Are supply management professionals responding in a timely fashion to internal customer inquiries?

- How often does the item received match the one ordered (with the standard being the contract or PO)?

- Are items that have not been received followed up on?

- Are competition requirements being met?

- For larger projects, how good is the forecast? How close was the actual price to the budgeted number?

- Is the organization using prompt payment discounts, if that is the organization's policy?

- Are the best transportation methods consistently being used?

- How do contract administrators gauge that contract requirements are being met? Are they accurately keeping payment records?

- Is receiving conducting incoming inspections for key components?

- Is technology used to its fullest advantage?

- Is supply management providing internal customers with appropriate information regarding new products, services and suppliers?

3) Corrective action process

The audit report presents findings (conclusions) based on observations. Audit reports are representations of fact. There should be no mention of blame, and the focus of the report should be on the audit standard. The number of findings varies with each audit. There should not be any surprises from the draft audit report presented in the closing meeting.

Even in award-winning organizations, there are normally areas in need of improvement. Internal auditors and regulatory auditors normally require a plan that outlines what steps are going to be taken to address audit findings. The corrective action required will vary depending on the magnitude and root cause of the problem. In general, the process will include establishing time frames for improvement, prioritizing the steps in the improvement plan, and conducting cost/benefit analysis to determine the appropriate level of resources to allocate to the corrective action plan implementation.

A) **Establishment of time frames** — Once a problem area is identified, it is necessary to establish time frames for corrective action. This may take the form of a final due date, along with milestones and time frames leading up to full implementation of the corrective action.

The supply management professional must be clear about the purpose of the corrective action. In some cases, the first step may be to take the time to determine the root cause of the problem and then to develop an action plan for dealing with the root cause. In other cases, interim measures may be taken to deal with symptoms of the real problem, while a plan is developed for identifying the root cause.

B) **Prioritization** — Whatever the process, prioritizing the steps in the implementation plan is critical. This process should include an understanding of the resources needed for the action and their availability.

C) **Cost/benefit analysis** — Corrective action must be cost-effective, given the expected benefits if the action is undertaken. A comparison of resources (people, time, equipment, money, etc.) and availability to the expected value (quantified in some way) should be performed. An ability to quantify the value of the benefits achieved is paramount. In most process improvements, this benefit is in the form of saving time. One of the most commonly used methods of quantifying savings is through activity-based cost (ABC) analysis. (See Task 2-E-2 for more information on ABC analysis.)

D) **Implementation** — Once it has been determined that the corrective action is cost-effective, it is time to take action. The supply management professional should set start and stop dates for taking corrective action, assign corrective action activities and advise the relevant stakeholders that corrective activities have been set in motion. These activities should be monitored to assure compliance.

E) **Validation** — After a pre-set amount of time has passed, the progress of the corrective action activities should be reviewed. This can be accomplished by comparing any progress that has been made against predetermined standards. In essence, the organization needs to make sure corrective action has resolved the issue found in the audit. If this is not the case, additional measures may need to be considered and implemented to assure any issue found in the audit is resolved.

4) Audit schedules and reports

The auditor's report is a formal opinion or disclaimer issued by the internal auditor or an independent external auditor as a result of an internal, external or self-inspection examination. The report is provided to the group that requested the audit — whether the organization's board of directors or the supply management department's senior leadership. Depending on the type of audit, the schedules included will vary. A financial audit will include various financial statements and accompanying notes.

BIBLIOGRAPHY

Adapted from the C.P.M. *Study Guide*, 7th edition, Institute for Supply Management®, Tempe, AZ, 2001.

Cavinato, J.L., A.E. Flynn, M.L. Harding, C.S. Lallatin, M.L. Peck, H.M. Pohlig, S.R. Sturzl and V. Tucker (Eds.). ISM *Glossary of Key Supply Management Terms*, 6th edition, Institute for Supply Management®, Tempe, AZ, 2014.

International Accounting Standards Board. www.ifrs.org, May 2013.

Johnson, P.F., Leenders, M. and A.E. Flynn. *Purchasing and Supply Management*, 14th edition, McGraw-Hill/Irwin, New York, 2010.

Planning

Task 2-E-1

Implement or use requirements planning (xRP — for example, Enterprise Resource Planning [ERP], Materials Requirements Planning [MRP], Manufacturing Resource Planning [MRPII], Distribution Requirements Planning [DRP and DRPII], Warehouse Management Systems [WMS]) to align supply management and operations activities to support organizational strategy.

Information technology advances continue to reshape the way supply management professionals conduct business and support an organization's strategy. Information systems tie together business operations, supply management and logistics with the supplier's organization and customer. Commonly used systems include enterprise resource planning (ERP), materials requirements planning (MRP), manufacturing resource planning (MRP II) and distribution requirements planning (DRP).

1) Key Principles of xRP

According to the ISM *Glossary* (2014), xRP is an acronym for "_____ requirements (or resource) planning" systems where the "x" may be materials, enterprise, manufacturing or distribution.

A) **Enterprise integration** — Dependent demand planning systems, based on the fundamental hierarchal linkages of materials requirements planning (MRP), have used the power of computers and communication systems to provide highly integrated and relatively easy to use software that gives high visibility across extensive portions of supply chains for an organization. The early integration of such systems (often called MRP II) provided the ability to provide plans for several key areas of the organization, but most of those were internal. More recent systems, often called enterprise resource planning systems (ERP), have expanded the ability to plan areas of the supply chain well beyond those included in the MRP II systems.

Materials requirements planning (MRP) — This is a system used to determine the quantity and timing requirements of dependent demand materials used in a manufacturing operation. Materials can be purchased externally or produced in-house. This computer-based system uses a master production schedule, bill of materials and current inventory data to determine current new requirements and timing (ISM *Glossary* 2014).

Enterprise integration provides the ability to plan and replenish inventory needs much better than basic reorder point systems by including actual orders rather than inventory levels. Enterprise systems integrate several basic data systems, including inventory, bills of material, master schedules (including both customer orders and forecasts), open orders and production scheduling systems. Using the master schedules generated in the master production schedule (MPS), the basic system expands the master schedule requirements, level by level, down the bill of materials. It will net the actual requirements by including the existing inventory levels (as well as future expected inventory levels, as captured in the purchase orders and production orders), and offset the requirements based on planned lead time. The primary output is a series of planned orders that can be used to generate production orders and purchase orders. Supply management provides a major source of information (including lead times and the open order database) and is a major user of the system, as many of the planned orders generated by the system can be used to develop purchase orders. A fundamental requirement for MRP to work effectively is having the key data maintained with a high level of accuracy, including timely inputs of transactions. The minimum data requirements to run a basic MRP system include:

- Inventory records

- Existing orders, both customer orders and purchase orders

- Bills of materials

- Lead times.

Manufacturing requirements planning II (MRP II) — This is a method for the effective planning of all resources used in a manufacturing organization. Ideally, it addresses operational planning in units and financial planning in dollars, and has a simulation capacity to answer "what if" questions. It is composed of a variety of functions — business planning, sales and operations planning, production planning, master production scheduling, material requirements planning, capacity requirements planning and the execution support systems for capacity and materials, all of which are linked. Manufacturing requirements planning is a direct outgrowth and extension of closed-loop materials resource planning (MRP).

Basic MRP systems are capacity insensitive. When the existing and planned orders from MRP are included in a capacity planning module, however, the planning system is greatly enhanced in several aspects, including:

- Orders can be "smoothed" and otherwise adjusted to lessen the impact on and cost for production work, transportation and supplier orders. This additional information can allow supply management professionals to work with suppliers to potentially decrease lead times and provide more accurate estimates for those lead times.

- The results of the capacity plans can be used to manage the master schedule more effectively, including the ability to meet customer orders more efficiently. The enhanced information can be used to time marketing approaches such as promotions, price changes or advertising campaigns.

- Requirements for and timing of capacities and material can be used to plan resource needs, including human resource needs and cash flows.

While adding these features to the basic MRP system greatly improves planning, MRP II does require additional information. As with basic MRP, the data systems that provide the information must be accurate and maintained in a timely manner. MRP II includes more functions in the organization, and as such can start to change the "culture" of the organization itself, including the need for more cross-functional integration and changing the performance measures and their relative priority in the organization's evaluation systems.

Distribution requirements planning (DRP) — The ISM *Glossary* (2014) defines DRP as the time-based demand from the distribution center to balance the customer fill rate against inventory investment.

DRP uses essentially the same logic as does MRP, but instead of planning requirements for production, DRP plans the net requirements on a central distribution point or a production facility by combining the net requirements from satellite warehouses or distribution centers. DRP, like MRP II, time-phases the requirements based on the lead time for replenishment of the product to these satellite centers. The information can be used to reduce costs of shipping, storage, packaging and receiving materials in the distribution center. The data from DRP can be used as an input to the Master Production Schedule (MPS) to aid in planning the production of inventory for the distribution system. As with MRP-based systems, purchase orders are an important input to the projected inventory system, and these DRP systems can be used to effectively plan purchasing requirements and supplier optimization.

Distribution resource planning (DRPII) — This is a time-phased computerized inventory system to replenish inventory in multi-echelon warehousing systems. It includes planning for warehouse space, manpower requirements, transportation alternatives and financial flows (ISM *Glossary* 2014).

Enterprise resource planning (ERP) — This refers to a particular type of computer software package that integrates various functions within an organization. It may be used to enable processes such as forecasting, materials management, procurement, accounting, finance, engineering and customer service.

B) **Data source consolidation** — As computer systems and information technologies improved, the fundamental concepts of MRP II were expanded to incorporate more aspects of the full enterprise including other plants, divisions, the corporate structure of the organization, suppliers and customers. These ERP systems are often designed to accommodate different languages and exchange rates for different currencies. As should be expected, these highly integrated software packages require many more data sources, expanding both the integration aspect of the organization and the pressure on the accuracy and timeliness of data. These systems tend to be complex and time-consuming to organize and implement because of their highly integrated nature. When implemented properly, however, they have the capability to provide a very powerful tool for an organization to plan, schedule and control virtually all aspects of production and all elements in the supply chain for that production.

C) **Information sharing** — Enterprisewide systems allow for the sharing and use of data by all business units in the organization. Things to consider with determining what information should be shared include: What information is available? How is the information accessed? Who should have access to what information? The sharing of information with key suppliers often leads to improved performance. After reviewing the supply base, the supply management professional should determine what information the suppliers need. Determine what information can be shared and under what conditions.

D) **Data integrity** — Assuring that the data entered into the enterprisewide system are accurate is always an issue. Managers make critical decisions based on reports generated by the system and are only as useful as the data used to generate them. Some indicators of poor data integrity include excessive inventory build-up, an increasing trend of part shortages and continuous decline in on-time performance. Once an organization implements a new ERP system, data cleanup should first take place. Some data can be cleaned up electronically while other data may have to be manually corrected. A good approach is to ask the data owners to review the system to assure their data has been successfully transferred. Then, ongoing monitoring must take place to assure data quality remains.

2) System development life cycle (SDLC)

System development life cycle (SDLC) is a method to develop, maintain and replace information systems. Typical phases in the SDLC are: analysis, design, development, integration and testing, implementation and maintenance.

A) **Analysis** —There are many systems and software programs available to assist in the effective management of an organization. While many of these systems can be effectively used in their basic out-of-the-box form, most organizations want and implement some customizing. The organization should, therefore, conduct a comprehensive analysis to determine the system or systems that will provide the optimal level of support at the minimal cost. Included in the analysis should be:

- Information output requirements, including level of detail, frequency of need and timing

- Existing data and information support systems

- Extent of integration required

- Capacity available, both labor and hardware.

B) **Design** — The analysis should define what the final systems should include, and these design parameters include:

- Data requirements, including level of detail, timing and accuracy

- Integration plan based on the extent and types of integration required

- Cost

- Implementation plan, including responsibilities and timing

- Capacity requirements, including labor and hardware

- Training plans.

Once the details of the design are developed, commercial software packages should be evaluated with respect to the ideal design parameters. In most cases, existing software packages, even if not perfectly matching the design parameters, are usually preferable to developing a software application internally because of timing and cost.

C) **Development** — The development phase involves buying or writing the code for any software designed uniquely for the organization. In some cases there are changes made to packaged software programs or "add-on" modules written to work with packaged software to meet the unique needs of the system designed and organizational requirements. In most customizations there will be an initial added cost to the software. The software may also need to be retrofitted each time the software company updates its product; the buying organization will have to pay for this retrofit. In addition, changes may need to be made throughout the organization to support the new system, including:

- Purchasing of necessary new hardware or communication systems

- Updating of policies, procedures and work instructions

- Developing/updating training programs

- Hiring any new employees needed to support the system

- Changing functional relationships as needed

- Implementing any new measurement or evaluation programs needed to support the new system.

D) **Testing** — If the analysis and design portion of the development are done properly, there are explicit criteria (measures) to determine if the implemented system is operating according to the design. The testing phase should include carefully operating the system under all expected operating conditions and evaluating the results against the criteria.

E) **Implementation** — Once the system is operating as expected, the software is put into operation and begins supporting business activities and decision-making. Immediate issues identified in the testing phase also are resolved at this time.

F) **Maintenance** — Maintenance and upkeep involve the day-to-day tasks required to operate and maintain the system. Common activities include software coding changes and corrections, reviews, and possibly a move to a new computer platform over time. Maintenance continues for the life of the system. Although not glamorous, these activities are necessary for optimal performance.

BIBLIOGRAPHY

Cavinato, J.L., A.E. Flynn, M.L. Harding, C.S. Lallatin, M.L. Peck, H.M. Pohlig, S.R. Sturzl and V. Tucker (Eds.). ISM *Glossary of Key Supply Management Terms*, 6th edition, Institute for Supply Management®, Tempe, AZ, 2014.

Develop, implement, maintain and monitor the forecasting, operations planning, scheduling and inventory control functions to ensure optimum use of capacity and resources.

Forecasting is an important activity in operations planning and provides input into production scheduling. Once production begins, inventory must be monitored and controlled to ensure suppliers have enough capacity to meet demand and resources are not over- or underutilized.

Supply management professionals engage in forecasting every day, though it generally involves routine projections of short-term activities and outcomes. These routine forecasts usually use one or more "judgmental" techniques, which are far more subjective than other, more advanced techniques. Sophisticated forecasting, particularly the involvement of multiple variables, requires the use of statistics and computer programs. In all cases, much consideration should be given to the selection of a proper forecasting method to ensure correct interpretation of results. It is imperative that the practitioner be knowledgeable in these areas and possess good judgment, as the forecasting technique selected must be appropriate for the application (Lewis 2000).

1) Replenishment/priority tool

Supply management professionals use a variety of methods and tools to automate and/or simplify the management of inventory.

A) **Supplier-managed inventory (SMI)/Vendor-managed inventory (VMI)** — This is an inventory management system that holds a supplier responsible for ensuring that stock is maintained at appropriate levels in the purchaser's facility and for replenishing items when these levels drop; sometimes referred to as vendor-managed inventory (ISM *Glossary* 2014).

B) **ABC analysis** — As defined in the ISM *Glossary* (2014), ABC analysis is the application of Pareto's Law, or the 80/20 rule, to define three categories — A, B and C. ABC analysis is used to determine the relative ratios between the number of items and the dollar value of the items purchased repetitively for stock; the number of purchase orders and the dollar value; and the number of suppliers and percent of spend. In most organizations, 10 percent to 20 percent of the items ("A" items) account for 70 percent to 80 percent of the investment; the next 15 percent to 25 percent of the items ("B" items) account for 10 percent to 20 percent of the investment; and the remaining 65 percent to 75 percent of the items ("C" items) account for 5 percent to 10 percent of the investment. Inventories, purchases and suppliers should be managed accordingly, with more emphasis placed on the strategic management of the "A" items and looser controls and less attention on "C" items.

The classifications are used to help indicate the degree of effort needed to maintain accuracy of records (a cost/benefit trade-off), including how much inventory accuracy error is allowed and how often cycle counting is done. In some cases a critical item (for example, one very difficult to obtain or with a long lead time) is artificially classified "A," even though the annualized dollar value is low.

C) **Reorder point systems** — A continuous review inventory control system is one in which an order is placed whenever a withdrawal brings the inventory position to a predetermined reorder point level (ISM *Glossary* 2014). The reorder point quantity is often based on the demand for the item during replenishment lead time.

D) **Fixed order period** — A fixed order interval inventory control system is one in which an item's inventory position is reviewed on a scheduled periodic basis rather than continuously. An order is placed at the end of each review, if appropriate, and the order quantity usually varies. In this system the time between replenishment orders is the trigger for reordering rather than the quantity in inventory acting as the reorder point. The fixed order period method has the advantage of not having to maintain perpetual inventory records, but because of that there is an increased risk of stockout if the demand for the inventory is unusually high before the replenishment time period is reached. The system is fairly popular if several items are ordered from a single supplier, as it more readily allows for consolidated transportation.

E) **Fixed order quantity** — A material replenishment system is one in which the size of the orders remains fixed, while the time interval between them changes, depending on how quickly the items are consumed.

Often used with a quantity-based reorder point system, this system attempts to order a quantity that will minimize total cost, as measured by the cost to order and the cost to maintain a given inventory level. Most of these fixed order systems are based on the basic economic order quantity (EOQ) calculations.

F) **Kanban** — This is a Japanese term meaning "signal." The signal is usually specific information (sometimes on a printed card and sometimes provided through electronic means such as a bar code) including part name, description, quantity and so on that signals a cycle of replenishment for production and materials. It is a variation of the quantity-based reorder point system. The system is often associated with lean production since many organizations that implement Kanban do so in conjunction with an aggressive campaign to reduce the order cost, allowing a much smaller economic order quantity.

G) **Buffer/safety stock** — Buffer and safety stock is additional inventory held as a buffer against uncertainties in demand or in the supply system. For example, safety stock inventory for demand is often calculated as the standard deviation of demand during lead time multiplied by the number of standard deviations that represent the desired percentage customer service level of the organization for the item.

H) **Obsolete/damaged/slow moving/aged** — The age of unsold or unused inventory is tracked and monitored. At some point, items may be designated as slow moving and are wasting an organization's assets through lost opportunity costs and additional carrying costs. Obsolete inventory is no longer usable to the organization, because the intended use no longer exists. Damaged inventory is no longer fit for its intended purpose. Both obsolete and slow moving inventory still would be considered usable, whereas damaged goods would not.

2) Scheduling processes

A) **Flow manufacturing** — The basic concept of flow manufacturing is very generic in that it implies an almost continuous production of product, as in the case of repetitive manufacturing. In recent years, however, it has taken on numerous connotations, implying pull production in conjunction with lean production methods, and even the application of synchronous production methods based on the Theory of Constraints. The implication is that product is made based on customer demand in daily schedules.

B) **Level scheduling** — As the name implies, level scheduling usually means a level use of capacity for the organization. There are two basic approaches to level scheduling while still meeting all or most customer demand, even if that demand is erratic. One method is with the use of inventory to absorb demand when it exceeds production allocated to a given product over a set period of time. The other approach uses lean production methods that will allow the organization to economically produce small lots of product using flexible capacity that can accommodate the production of a wide range of product.

C) **Package optimization** — Packaging optimization attempts to minimize waste of packaging materials. It requires the analysis of the product and shipping environment to accommodate such aspects as product value (cost/benefit trade-off analysis), physical product characteristics, safety, mode of transportation, reuse of packaging materials and availability of materials.

D) **Shared visibility into inventory** — Modern supply chain techniques imply the synchronization of material production and flow throughout the supply chain. As such, it is important that each organization maximizes the visibility of customer demand as well as inventory in its own organization and in the supplier and customer organizations. The organization can more effectively plan production and distribution of their products to maximize customer service with the least inventory, transportation or other costs in the supply chain.

E) **Bullwhip effect** — As customers at the end of a supply chain (final consumption) need replacement product, the replacement requirement may be fairly small in quantity over a given time period. As that need progresses upstream in the supply chain, however, timing of production and transportation as well as lot sizing requirements in both production and transportation may multiply the requirement for production and shipping. That impact can often be magnified the further upstream one goes through the supply chain. Like a bull whip (where a small "flick" of the wrist can produce a very large impact at the end of the whip), a small need downstream in a supply chain can produce large fluctuations in need further upstream. Supply chain visibility and synchronization minimize this effect and the associated impacts.

3) Capacity utilization techniques

A) **Sales forecasts** — One of the major uses of sales forecasts is to help organizations to effectively plan the use of capacity in such a way that total costs are minimized while customer service is maximized. This is often done by inputting those forecasts into a sales and operations plan, which is really a process of analysis and tradeoffs across virtually all functions of the organization to establish the proper level of various resources needed at various times to meet the plan and projected demand.

B) **Implementation schedule** — When execution of a plan is taking place (usually based on actual customer orders rather than on a forecast), the organization must fine tune the utilization of capacity since forecasts are seldom absolutely correct and production may be ahead of or behind schedule for a number of reasons. Tracking the order load on the capacity and the projected available capacity allows the organization to adjust the use (the use of overtime, for example) for short time periods in the future.

C) **Supplier capacity analysis** — Supply management organizations must ensure that suppliers have enough capacity to meet their demands. The process begins by creating a supply forecast to determine if enough materials, parts and resources will be available to the buying organization in sufficient quantities to meet its production and service delivery requirements. At the same time, the organization needs to consider economic conditions and trends that could affect supplier capacity such as uncertain labor conditions, restraint on capital, new environmental laws, inflation or changing trade rules or regulations.

BIBLIOGRAPHY:

Cavinato, J.L., A.E. Flynn, M.L. Harding, C.S. Lallatin, M.L. Peck, H.M. Pohlig, S.R. Sturzl and V. Tucker (Eds.). ISM *Glossary of Key Supply Management Terms*, 6th edition, Institute for Supply Management®, Tempe, AZ, 2014.

Lewis, H.E. "Using Forecasting to Foresee Change," *Purchasing Today*®, (11:10), October 2000, p. 8.

Matthews, D.L. and L.L. Stanley. *Effective Supply Management Performance*, Institute for Supply Management®, Tempe, AZ, 2014.

Product and Service Development

Task 2-F-1

Participate in product/service development or specification/requirement changes that support organizational merchandising and marketing efforts to meet customer needs.

New product or service development (NPD/NSD) is a key source of competitive advantage for organizations, requiring the design of better, higher quality products and services and bringing them quickly to market. Organizations today can make use of information technology to bring individual departments together as teams to work on releasing new products or services. Supply management plays a key role in a new product handover to production, or the selection and coordination of suppliers for a new service offering.

1) Innovative and integrated product development process

A) **Customer requirements** — A customer requirement may present a problem to be solved. The requirements of the customer may be expressed or may be yet to be articulated, and represent new product or service development opportunities for the organization.

A needs analysis is important to understanding the customer's needs and wants. It is described in customer terms, and the organization then needs to develop a commercially viable solution. There are four key pieces of information that can be obtained from customers: (1) What is the problem? (2) Who has the problem? (3) How important is the problem's solution to the customer? (4) How valuable is the problem's solution to the customer?

B) **Product development teams** — Product development teams are responsible for finding solutions for customers or generating new ideas. The size of the team can range from a few to hundreds of members. Generally, the larger the team, the more inefficiencies can occur including communication problems and higher administrative costs. Team size should depend on the scope of the project.

These teams should be cross-functional in nature. Cross-functional teams help ensure the new product is designed taking into consideration manufacturability, procurability, reliability, maintainability, schedulability and marketability, in the early stages. Such considerations help avoid errors that waste time and resources later in the product life cycle. Involvement of back office operations staff, customers, front-line staff and suppliers is similarly critical. A consistent approach to new service development encompassing all relevant disciplines is critically important given the need to manage the more intangible aspects of service delivery and controlling contact with customers. Diverse backgrounds also allow for a broader base of knowledge, contacts and sources of information, which typically leads to greater innovation and solutions to potential design issues.

A critical practice in NPD/NSD is the use of concurrent engineering to capture input and knowledge from key stakeholders, internal and external. Concurrent engineering, typically employed via cross-functional teams, has been shown to be faster, cheaper and better for product and service development than serial alternatives.

C) **Cost management** — When a product is developed, the new product development team needs to keep pricing in mind and consider not only whether the customer will purchase this product but at what price. Organizations need to set the target cost based on the expected price and desired profit. The target cost is calculated as follows:

Target cost = Expected price - desired profit.

To meet a target cost likely will require some cost management activities, such as performing a cost trade-off analysis. This probably will involve design, engineering, marketing and others in negotiating on design specifications, materials and manufacturing processes to be used to reach the target cost. Also, the supply management organization may have to work with any other suppliers involved in the production of the product in an effort to reduce their prices to an acceptable level.

D) **Early purchasing involvement (EPI)** — Even before using early supplier involvement (ESI), the procurement group should be involved in the product and service development and design process. Procurement brings insight into supply market conditions, availability of materials and services, and potential sources of supply. Supply management also is able to apply such tools as value engineering and analysis, and standardization to specification development.

E) **Early supplier involvement (ESI)** — Early supplier involvement (ESI) is a practice that brings together one or more selected suppliers with the organization's product or service design team early in the product development process. The objective is to use the supplier's expertise and experience in developing a product or service specification that is designed for effective and efficient product rollout (ISM *Glossary* 2014). Manufacturing and services organizations benefit from following the general rule of involving key suppliers earlier and more extensively in the new product or service development process, and can generate significant gains in product design, service delivery and customer satisfaction.

F) **Process design integration** — When a new product is planned for market launch, the processes required to make the new product should be simultaneously considered. This step requires integrating the new process for the product into existing operations. Design of products (materials, components) has considerable cost impact on making them fit with current equipment and setup process.

G) **Design process execution** — After all aspects of the product and process design have been addressed, the design team completes the design. The supply management professional's role will be to begin the procurement of any materials and tooling needed for the design.

H) **Validation and testing** — Once the design is fully developed, it should be validated and tested where it will typically be used to determine if it will perform as desired and to verify customer interest. Testing may take place in a laboratory, using a survey, through interviews with a focus group of customers, by introducing it at a trade show, or by making a small quantity and placing it in a test market to estimate product acceptance. At this stage the product may either be shelved or adjustments will be made as necessary before general release to the marketplace.

2) Role of supply management in product or service design teams

A) **Research and development** — Before the design drawings and specifications are released, there has to be a dialog between the designer/ internal customer and the supply management department. Both bring desirable information to the table. The supply management professional's knowledge of the supply markets allows the sharing of information about service, product or material availability, as well as information regarding new developments on the horizon. Working together improves speed of release, cost-effectiveness and total quality for a new initiative.

B) **Substitution** — Supply management may be able to recommend services, parts or materials that meet functional requirements at the lowest practicable cost. Often suppliers can recommend newer or alternative solutions that provide the same function.

C) **Product innovation** — Supply management is responsible for maintaining and developing relationships with suppliers that result in their sharing information on innovations with the supply management professional's organization. If such relationships are carefully cultivated, suppliers may recommend new products or services on the market that enable the designer or internal customer to make inventive or resourceful changes.

D) **Contracting for design services** — During the design phase, scarce project resources (for example, time of designers and engineers, computer capacity) can often delay release of a product into the marketplace. Supply management can contract with outside services to help ensure that each project stays on target. Design services that may be contracted include circuit design, software development and programming, prototype machine and assembly, graphic design, technical writing, modeling, testing and equipment rental.

E) **Qualified product lists (QPL)** — The speed of the entire design process is dependent on the weakest link in the process. Consequently, it is advisable to avoid parts or processes that may impede the smooth flow of the operation. Supply management can assist design and engineering teams by calling attention to parts that are on a qualified products list and those that may have long or unstable lead times.

F) **Early supplier involvement (ESI)** —There are a number of areas in which supply management can play an important part in the early supplier involvement (ESI) process.

Manufacturing process — Knowledge of both the supplier's and the customer's manufacturing procedures is important to the development of the most effective process to produce a product. Supply management professionals and suppliers working together can eliminate many cost redundancies. For example, an organization can buy a product that is partially completed and introduce it to its process at an earlier stage; or a supplier can take on some of the customer's operations if doing so would lead to lower costs and improved quality. The supply management organization has a greater opportunity to come up with cost efficiencies if it understands the supplier's processes. Significant time and money can be saved if the supplier is "on the team" early in the development of the manufacturing process. Suppliers can suggest the type of equipment that might be more compatible with their processes. This fosters a more strategic relationship with the supplier.

Capital acquisitions budget — Supply management can make the most significant contribution to the budget/approval process if it is involved early with engineering, manufacturing or the internal customer that is developing a new product or service. This involvement is called early procurement involvement (EPI). The supply management professional who is aware of a need for a capital asset can develop a list of suppliers that can satisfy that need. This not only speeds up the development of a capital project proposal, but also shortens the later acquisition process. Forecasting a need for equipment or facilities will allow potential suppliers to allocate manufacturing or human resources time in advance of the need. This will also assist in shortening the acquisition for long lead time items. Capital asset availability can provide a competitive advantage in new product or service introduction.

Product or service development/implementation — Suppliers can be of assistance in early product development by providing prototypes, models or preproduction samples for testing and/or use in the customer's product development cycle. Suppliers can be equally helpful in the implementation of a new or changing service. Good communication and feedback between the customer and the supplier is important if early product or service development efforts are to provide maximum value.

Suppliers can provide useful insight into the costs of manufacturing a product or providing a service and realistic assessments of what the product or service development will entail before the product or service is introduced into the market or procured by the supply management organization. Having cost projections from a supplier on a new product or service can keep an organization from making expensive errors in judgment and enhance the decision-making ability of the buying organization.

Quality — Early involvement of suppliers in the development of specifications for products and processes will help to reduce the costs of quality of a product or service. Suppliers can help with the development of quality requirements that will serve the customer in the most effective manner. If suppliers are made aware of a customer's needs, they can prepare their organizations to satisfy those needs through human resource development and training, process development and capability studies, and equipment acquisition. Quality is the result of preplanning and preparation. Suppliers that have knowledge of quality requirements can eliminate problems that lead to rejections or rework at later stages.

Availability — Suppliers must have the capacity to serve a customer's needs. If a supplier is aware of forecasted needs, it can then inform the potential customer what support it can provide. Supply management professionals are responsible for working with their internal customers to provide forecasted data to the supplier base. This will help eliminate future supplier delivery problems.

Technology — Supplier expertise in the technology arena can be helpful to a design person and will increase the chances of producing a quality and cost-effective product early in the design/marketing cycle. Supplier technological understanding may influence final material selection and many other areas, especially when the designer does not have a broad knowledge of technological advances occurring in the marketplace. Supply management can assist in the transfer of information by bringing together an organization's technical staff with the supplier's technologically qualified personnel. However, such exchanges can take place only if the supplier believes there is a chance to develop future business. Early in the process, supply management and the internal design stakeholder's group should choose a group of suppliers with which they are willing to work. Supply management professionals must understand that suppliers share information on advances in technology and related intelligence on a selected basis.

Design — Suppliers can provide key elements to a product design, based on their experience in serving a particular market. Supply management professionals who have long-term relationships with suppliers can often have their designers seek the advice of suppliers, with the understanding that the supplier's technology and designs must be protected. Usually a nondisclosure agreement (NDA) is signed by both parties to ensure confidentiality. It is important the supplier also have a reasonable opportunity to gain business from this activity.

Product co-development — Using suppliers in the co-development of a product or service provides for a sharing of development costs. This normally implies there is a formal agreement regarding future business that may result from the development. This agreement can take many forms. For example, the organization can pay the supplier for the development costs, pay a royalty on each item sold or guarantee future business. Co-development spreads the risk to more than one organization. It implies that the rewards will be shared. Often this is the only way a supplier will share proprietary technology.

Cycle time — Total cycle time can be reduced by the early development of relationships with suppliers. These relationships can assist with the elimination of redundancies in product development, manufacturing and distribution processes. These relationships can assist in the introduction of new or changing services. Once the product, process or service is in place, the cycle required to provide the ultimate customer with the desired product can be improved on a continuous basis.

G) **Sourcing and cost profitability issues** — Supply management can become involved up front to make sure all potential costs are identified accurately early in a product or service design project. With its knowledge of suppliers' products, services and know-how, supply management is in a position to suggest materials and component substitutions, items ripe for standardization, how processes might be modified, and if specifications are clearly and effectively written, to enhance competition. Use of such information, and the application of cost-saving concepts, ensures that supply management is adding value and contributing to the successful decision-making processes within the organization.

H) **Target costing** — This concept is used in supply management to identify the allowable price for a supplier's product or service, which starts with the selling price of the buyer's end product, or service for its end product, or service in the marketplace, and subtracting out the required profit. The amount remaining is the total that it can cost the organization to make that product or to perform that service, including materials. This cost is allocated among purchases and internal costs. The result is the target cost for each item. Supply management then works with suppliers to ensure their prices come in at or below the target cost. Further analysis and negotiation is done to remove costs from the buyer's and the seller's operations to reduce the price to the acceptable target level (ISM *Glossary* 2014).

BIBLIOGRAPHY

Adapted from the C.P.M. *Study Guide*, 7th edition, Institute for Supply Management®, Tempe, AZ, 2001.

Cavinato, J.L., A.E. Flynn, M.L. Harding, C.S. Lallatin, M.L. Peck, H.M. Pohlig, S.R. Sturzl and V. Tucker (Eds.). ISM *Glossary of Key Supply Management Terms*, 6th edition, Institute for Supply Management®, Tempe, AZ, 2014.

Handfield, R.B., G.L. Ragatz, K.J. Petersen and R.M. Monczka. "Involving Suppliers in New Product Development," *California Management Review*, (42:1), 1999, pp. 59-82.

Hull, F.M. "Innovation Strategy and the Impact of a Composite Model of Service Product Development on Performance," *Journal of Service Research*, (7:2), 2004, pp. 167-180.

Wagner, S.M. and M. Hoegl. "Involving Suppliers in Product Development: Insights from R&D Directors and Project Managers," *Industrial Marketing Management*, (35:8), 2006, pp. 936-943.

Manage ramp-up strategy and implementation to full-scale production for new product or service introductions.

Time to market has been perceived as a critical source of competitive advantage that enables organizations to achieve fast payback on their new product development and production investments, and to gain a market leading position from early entry. However, these advantages depend on time-to-volume, or "ramp-up." Ramp-up is the period during which the manufacturing process makes the transition from zero to full-scale production at targeted levels of cost and quality. It may take weeks or even months to reach this point as operators must learn the new process, and process problems are identified and fixed.

1) Sales projections

Sales projections are critical to achieve effective ramp-up. Poor forecasting can lead to involuntary downtime as suppliers cannot, or have not, supplied enough of the critical components. Other times, the supply management professional may rely on the supplier to handle problems caused by poor sales forecasts.

2) Staffing requirements

Ramp-up projects operate most effectively within a cross-functional and cross-location team structure. As production moves from the pilot environment to volume production, cooperation among people and departments is critical.

3) Operations capacity and capabilities

A) **Operations flexibility and response time** — Ramp-up is characterized by high variability and uncertainty, with conflicts in managing short cycle times and fast throughput increases. Operations flexibility to achieve a fast entry strategy may be achieved through mechanisms such as computer-aided-design/computer-aided-manufacturing (CAD/CAM), design for manufacturing and aggregate project planning.

B) **Equipment and labor capabilities** — During ramp-up, new equipment needs to be delivered, hooked up, installed and aligned with the right processes. For first-time production, this may also require detailed experiments and analyses to prove process capability prior to release of any product. Similarly, skilled labor in production engineers is required to undertake rapid problem-solving to build knowledge of the process and improve yield rates.

4) Supply chain readiness

A) **Logistics/distribution capabilities**

Efficient logistics networks are key to rapid ramp-up and to ensure that materials arrive on production lines on the desired schedule. Rapid logistics may also help keep to the schedule when supplier shortages occur as components may be shifted from locations in surplus to another in deficit.

B) **Supplier capability/capacity analysis**

Although a supplier may have an innovative technology, it may not be able to meet the requirements for capacity, delivery, quality and cost. New, innovative suppliers are typically small and have limited production capacity. In some cases, the buyer may represent 50 percent or more of a small supplier's annual revenue. Supply management professionals must be mindful of not only the technological aspects of product design but also of commercial issues of capacity and ramp-up.

1.0) **Tooling** — Tooling and capacity investment decisions typically have long lead times and as such must be made early. Once made, they have a lasting impact. A decision to invest too little in tooling and capacity can take a long time to correct, which carries a high opportunity cost. A decision to invest too much in tooling and capacity can significantly increase the per-unit cost of the component or module. Organizations may review the tooling capacity of their suppliers prior to launch to ensure that all production tooling is in place to meet expected demand for the new product.

2.0) **Prototype qualification** — Testing and evaluation of prototypes for minimal technical requirements is critical for meeting long-term cost and performance targets. Qualification prototype refers to building and verifying the product, per final design prints.

C) **Lead time and inventory planning**

A key challenge of ramp-up is ensuring the supply chain maintains pace with the volume growth. Particularly in a global production network, organizations may continue needing to source from existing suppliers with longer lead times to meet planned inventory levels.

BIBLIOGRAPHY

Clawson, R.T. "Controlling the Manufacturing Start-up," *Harvard Business Review*, 63, 1985, pp. 6-20.

Terwiesch, C., R. E. Bohn and K. S. Chea. "International Product Transfer and Production Ramp-up: A Case Study from the Data Storage Industry," *R&D Management*, (31:4), 2001, pp. 435-451.

Project Management

Perform project management activities representing the supply management organization.

Supply management and project management are integrally related. Supply management is defined as the identification, acquisition, access, positioning, management of resources and related capabilities the organization needs or potentially needs, in the attainment of its strategic objectives (ISM *Glossary* 2014). Supply management components include the following (ISM 2012):

1. Disposition/Investment Recovery

2. Distribution

3. Inventory Control

4. Logistics

5. Manufacturing Supervision

6. Materials Management

7. Operations

8. Packaging

9. Procurement/Purchasing

10. Product/Service Development

11. Quality

12. Receiving

13. Strategic Sourcing

14. Transportation/Traffic/Shipping

15. Warehousing/Stores.

Project management, on the other hand, is defined as the process of coordinating the organization, planning, scheduling, controlling, monitoring and evaluating of activities so that the objectives of a project are met (ISM *Glossary* 2014). Thus, project management can be considered a method or approach for conducting many supply management activities.

Supply management and project management can be viewed from two perspectives. First, supply management activities are typically executed as projects. For example, the supply management department of a high-tech computer organization may be faced with establishing a second source of supply for a critical commodity, material or service. This supply management activity, establishing a second source of supply, may be treated as a project within the organization, and the use of project management processes will be instrumental in the success of this effort. Second, many projects managed by an organization typically require some extent of supply management activities, such as sourcing in support of a larger enterprisewide project. For example, a technology services organization may have received a contract to source and install new security gates as part of an automated border solution for an international airport. The fulfillment of the contract requirements will be considered a major project, which includes some supply management activities, such as the negotiation and award of a subcontract for the development and installation of the gates.

Given these two perspectives, supply management and project management continue to be closely related. Regardless of the perspective one takes on project management, all project life cycle activities typically fall into one of the five project management process groups — initiation, planning, execution, monitoring and controlling, and closing. This task will discuss these project management process groups as they relate to supply management activities.

1) Project initiation

These processes are related to defining and authorizing the project or project phase (PMI 2013). For supply management activities, project initiation processes typically focus on needs identification or problem definition, which involves determining project feasibility, proposing a project solution and obtaining project approval and authorization.

A) **Project scope analysis** — Someone — an individual, a department, senior management or the CEO — generally initiates a project because some complex issue is perceived to affect the organization's ability to operate effectively. Before the project is approved, however, some analysis should be conducted to determine if there is a problem to be solved and if so, if the recommended project will provide a solution. These analyses include the following:

1.0 **Strength, weaknesses, opportunity, threats (SWOT) analysis** — SWOT analysis is a strategic planning approach to assessing an organization's strengths, weaknesses, opportunities and threats. A form of risk analysis, this assessment helps senior management evaluate the current conditions internally and externally that triggered the need for a given project (Matthews and Stanley 2014). See Tasks 1-F-1, 2-A-1, 2-C-2 and 3-A-2 for additional discussions on SWOT analysis.

2.0 **Kepner-Tregoe rational process analysis** — Kepner-Tregoe is defined as systematic procedures developed by Charles H. Kepner and Benjamin B. Tregoe to apply critical thinking to information, data and experience for the purpose of solving problems, making decisions, anticipating future problems and appraising situations (ISM *Glossary* 2014). Kepner-Tregoe includes four steps: situational appraisal, problem analysis, decision analysis and potential problem/opportunity analysis. Based on the analysis, the possible causes of the problem can be determined and the organization can then develop a project to resolve the problem.

3.0 **Six Sigma process analysis** — Six Sigma is an approach used to systematically improve processes by eliminating defects or non-value-added activities. Existing processes are often affected by a new project, so the use of Six Sigma tools may become part of the project scope.

4.0 **Business case analysis** — This is an approach to analyzing a business case for a proposed project. A business case is a structured proposal for business improvement that functions as a decision package for organizational decision-makers (ISM *Glossary* 2014). The business case should include the reasons for the proposed project, estimated costs, expected benefits, an analysis of alternatives to the project and the expected risks.

5.0 **Alternative analysis** — This is the part of a business case analysis that analyzes the various alternatives to a proposed project.

6.0 **Project feasibility analysis** — This is a preliminary analysis to determine the feasibility of a proposed project prior to the project being approved. One section of the feasibility analysis would include the financial evaluation of the proposed project using such tools as net present value, internal rate of return and payback period calculations.

    6.1 **Net present value (NPV), internal rate of return (IRR), payback** — NPV analysis is a capital budgeting technique used to equate the discounted cash flows against the initial investment for the project (Kerzner 2013).

    IRR analysis is a capital budgeting technique that calculates the discount rate that equates the discounted cash flows of the project with the initial investment (Kerzner 2013).

    Payback period analysis is the period of time needed for a

project to recover its initial investment, based on the cash inflows (Kerzner 2013).

7.0 **Stakeholder analysis** — This is an analysis of the stakeholders involved in a proposed project. Stakeholders may include customers, sponsors, project team members, and anybody else who may have an interest in the outcome of the project.

Once the need or requirement has been identified and the project is selected, it is important the organization develop a project charter, which formally authorizes the project, designates the project manager and project team, and commits sufficient resources to the project effort.

8.0 **Project charter** — The project charter is the document that formally authorizes the formation of the project and provides the project manager with the authority needed to execute the project activities (PMBOK 2008).

8.1 **Project charter approval process** — The project charter approval process is conducted as a result of the project alternative analysis and project selection process (PMBOK 2008). The project charter is issued by the project sponsor, typically external to the project organization. The project sponsor should be high enough in the organization appropriate to the level of funding needed for the project.

2) Project planning

These processes define project objectives and plan the course required to obtain the project's scope and objectives (PMI 2013). For supply management-related projects such as major procurement actions, project planning involves supply management activities such as procurement planning and solicitation planning.

A) **Procurement planning process** — Procurement planning involves the process of identifying which business needs can be best met by procuring products or services outside the organization. This process involves determining whether to procure, how to procure, what to procure, how much to procure and when to procure (Garrett and Rendon 2005). This process includes:

1.0 **Solicitation planning process** — Once supply management has determined that outside resources will be needed to complete a project, potential suppliers need to be identified. Solicitation planning involves the process of determining what will be needed to support the solicitation. This process involves documenting project requirements and identifying potential sources (Garrett and Rendon 2005). This process includes:

- Determining contract type — Contracts are typically categorized by cost, fixed price, and time and materials. More on types of contracts can be found in Task 1-A-4.

- Determining the type of solicitation — There are a number of solicitation documents available to communicate to the supplier including an invitation for bid, request for quotation or request for proposal. A deeper discussion of these documents can be found in Task 1-A-1.

- Determining proposal evaluation criteria and contract award strategy — Evaluation criteria are those used to evaluate the supplier's bids or proposals. The contract award strategy includes lowest price/technically acceptable, or other-than-the-lowest-priced bid, based on the evaluation criteria.

- Structuring contract terms and conditions — The terms and conditions refer to the clauses in the contract that govern the contractor's and buyer's obligations in performing the contract.

- Finalizing solicitation — Work breakdown structure (WBS) is a project management technique for defining and organizing the total scope of a project using a hierarchal tree structure. A well-designed WBS describes planned outcomes, not actions. The statement of work (SOW) outlines the specific services a contractor is expected to perform and is discussed below in section 2.1.

2.0 **Scope development** — The requirement or scope of a project is a description of the work to be accomplished in the project. It describes the nature and extent of the project and outlines the conditions under which the work is to be performed.

2.1 **Statement (or scope) of work (SOW)** — The SOW is the part of the solicitation documents that describes the part of the project that will be accomplished by the supplier. The SOW generally indicates the type, level and quality of service, as well as the time schedule required. See Task 1-A-1 for more information on SOW.

3.0 Project team roles and responsibilities — Based on the SOW and the related work breakdown structure, the project team must be assigned specific roles and responsibilities for performing the project.

3.1 Responsibility assignment matrix (RAM) — The RAM is a tool used to assign project team members their specific roles and responsibilities with respect to the project effort. The RAM typically assigns project team members to specific sections of the project work breakdown structure (WBS).

4.0 Budget development — The budget is the cost estimate, broken down by cost categories and the WBS elements for performing the activities of the project.

5.0 Schedule development — The schedule is a time-phased plan for performing the activities of the project. The time-phased spending plan is a planned schedule for incurring the estimated costs associated with the project budget.

5.1 Critical path — The critical path is generally the path of the network of project activities that determines the length of the project schedule.

6.0 Risk management — Risk management is the process used by the project team for conducting risk planning, risk identification, risk analysis, risk response planning, and risk monitoring and control throughout the life of the project. See Exam 3, Section 3-B for a further discussion on risk.

6.1 Risk matrix — The risk matrix is a risk analysis tool for assessing a risk based on an event's probability of occurring and the impact of that risk event.

7.0 Organizational structures — Organizational structures for the project can include functional, matrix and projectized types of organizational structures.

7.1 Functional, matrix, projectized — Projects can be performed by entities organized in a functional organizational structure in which departments are based on functional areas (accounting, engineering, finance, supply management, marketing).

A matrixed organizational structure reflects project roles, responsibilities and authority shared by functional department members and project managers.

A projectized organizational structure has greater degrees of independence and authority, with the project manager having full authority over the project team members.

8.0 **Project plan approval process** — The project plan approval process involves the approval of all projects to include the project budget, schedule and performance requirement. The project plan establishes the project baseline, in terms of cost, schedule and performance objectives.

This project baseline will then be used to measure actual project progress against project planned estimates.

3) Project execution

The processes discussed in this section integrate people and resources to carry out the project effort (PMI 2013). For supply management activities such as procurement and contracting, project execution involves implementing the supply management plans developed during project planning. This can involve executing the solicitation and source selection phases of the procurement process.

A) **Solicitation process** — The solicitation process involves obtaining information (bids and proposals) from the prospective suppliers on how project needs can be met (Garrett and Rendon 2005). This process includes:

- **Conduct pre-proposal conference** — A pre-proposal conference is typically conducted after the solicitation document is issued but before contractor proposals are received. This conference is used to answer any questions that interested offerors may have on the solicitation documents or the project.

- **Conduct advertising, if applicable** — Many organizations will advertise supply management project opportunities so they can have access to the latest technologies and market capabilities. Many government agencies (city, county, state and federal) are required by law to advertise some procurement opportunities.

- **Develop and maintain qualified bidders list** — Qualified bidders are those suppliers that have met a certain level of qualifications (quality, technical, etc.) as required by the buying organization.

1.0 **Source selection process** — The source selection process involves receiving bids or proposals and applying the proposal evaluation criteria to select a supplier (Garrett and Rendon 2005). This process includes:

- Apply evaluation criteria to management, cost and technical bids or proposals.

- Evaluate the bids or proposals based on the evaluation criteria stated in the solicitation document.

- Negotiate with suppliers.

- Execute contract award strategy.

- Based on the proposal/bid evaluation, award the contract using the contract award strategy stated in the solicitation document.

2.0 **Project team management** — For supply management activities, project monitoring and controlling involves managing the project team. This involves ensuring proper communication flow among project team members as well as generating project performance reports for use in measuring project performance.

3.0 **Change management** — Change management as defined in the ISM *Glossary* (2014) involves making changes in a planned or systematic fashion through the use of methods, models and practices common to the multidisciplinary body of knowledge surrounding the task of managing planned or unplanned change. Change management involves managing the changes that occur during the project, and administering the contract with the contractor. Changes to the initial project plan and baseline (cost, schedule and performance) objectives may occur during the project activities. Ensuring a controlled and disciplined change management process during project monitoring and control is essential to project success. Change management includes ensuring a disciplined project change control process.

4) Project monitoring and control

These processes measure and monitor the project effort to identify variances from the project plan so that corrective actions can be implemented (PMI 2013). This involves the contract administration phase of the procurement process.

A) **Contract administration process** — The contract administration process involves ensuring that each party's performance meets the contractual requirements (Garrett and Rendon 2005). This process includes conducting a pre-performance conference. A pre-performance conference is conducted after contract award but prior to contractor performance as an activity to kick off the project effort with the selected contractor. This is typically a project kickoff meeting to establish project protocols with the selected contractor.

1.0 Performance measurement tools — Earned value management, schedule analysis and budget analysis are used to measure the contractor's performance.

> **1.1 Earned value management, schedule analysis, budget analysis** — The earned value management (EVM) approach is an integrated method for assessing the supplier's project effort in terms of meeting cost, schedule and performance objectives. EVM calculates cost variance, schedule variance and the amount of earned value, based on work performed, costs incurred and schedule used. Using these metrics, EVM can then determine cost performance and schedule performance indices as well as estimate at completion.
>
> Schedule analysis compares planned schedule with actual schedule status. The results of schedule analysis include a determination of schedule variance.
>
> Budget analysis compares planned budget estimates with actual budget estimates. The results of budget analysis include a determination of cost variance.

2.0 Change control processes — A project/contract change control process is needed to control changes to the project baseline (cost, schedule and performance objectives), contract SOW, and terms and conditions (see change management information, above).

3.0 Risk monitoring process — Project management includes conducting risk management activities to monitor and control project risk. Risk monitoring and control use various techniques such as earned value management, schedule analysis and budget analysis. These techniques are used to assess the results of executed risk responses, or the identification of any new or emerging project risks.

4.0 Performance management reporting — Performance management reporting involves managing and reporting the supplier's cost, schedule and performance results of the contract effort. This reporting is used to monitor and control the project's progression through the project life cycle. At each project milestone review, the project status, as reported in the performance management reports, is used to assess the project performance and determine if the project should proceed to the next milestone.

  4.1 **Project constraints (scope, quality, schedule, budget, resources, risk)** — The project constraints of scope, quality, schedule, budget, resources and risk are the parameters of the project objectives that must be managed by the project team (PMBOK 2008). The project status is compared to a project baseline to determine if the project is progressing within the project constraints.

  4.2 **Milestone reviews** — Project milestones are used to review project progress at specific events in the project life cycle. Milestone reviews may be used to approve the advancement of the project into the next phase of the project.

 5.0 **Project management software programs** — Complex projects typically need formal and disciplined project management processes. These processes are usually supplemented with the use of project management software programs to aid in the initiating, planning, execution, monitoring and controlling, and closing of projects.

5) Project closure

Project closure processes formalize the acceptance of the project effort, either a product or service, and bring the project to an end (PMI 2013). For supply management activities such as procurement and contracting, project closing involves formally closing the project activities related to the contract, and documenting the project and contract files to reflect the project results. This involves conducting contract closeout activities.

 A) **Contract closeout processes** — Contract closeout is the process of verifying that all administrative matters are concluded on a contract that is otherwise physically complete (Garrett and Rendon 2005). This process includes:

  1.0 **Property dispositions process** — Projects may involve the use of property and equipment from other organizations. Project closure activities include the disposition of project property in accordance with organizational or contractual requirements.

  2.0 **Final product/service acceptance** — Final product/service acceptance includes the buying organization's processes and documentation related to the receipt and final acceptance of the contractor's products and services, as specified in the contract.

  3.0 **Final payment process** — Final payment process includes the buying organization's processes and documentation related to executing the final payment for the contractor's products and services, as specified in the seller's invoice and in the contract.

B) **Best practice and lessons learned identification** — A database of project and contract best practices (what worked well) and lessons learned (what did not work well) should be established to help the organization plan and manage future projects and to improve project management processes.

C) **Post project audit procedure** — A project audit is typically conducted to assess the completed project in terms of project methods, procedures, records, properties, budgets, actual costs and contractor performance.

BIBLIOGRAPHY

Cavinato, J.L., A.E. Flynn, M.L. Harding, C.S. Lallatin, M.L. Peck, H.M. Pohlig, S.R. Sturzl and V. Tucker (Eds.). ISM *Glossary of Key Supply Management Terms*, 6th edition, Institute for Supply Management®, Tempe, AZ, 2014.

Garrett, G.A. and R.G. Rendon. *Contract Management: Organizational Assessment Tools*, National Contract Management Association, 2005.

Project Management Institute. "A G uide to the Project Management Body of Knowledge (PMBOK®)," Project Management Institute, Inc., 5th edition, 2013. Copyright and all rights reserved. Material from this publication has been reproduced with the permission of PMI.

Kerzner, H. *Project Management: A Systems Approach to Planning, Scheduling, and Controlling*, 11th edition, Wiley, 2013.

Implement a continuous improvement process within the supply chain in accordance with organizational objectives.

Continuous improvement is critical to the success of the organization's supply management program. As an organization's supply management activities increase in importance in this ever-changing business environment, these organizations will continue to look at continuous improvement programs as a means of achieving and maintaining their supply management competitive advantage. Continuous improvement initiatives can be applied to many of the various supply management components such as disposition/investment recovery, distribution, inventory control, logistics, management supervision, manufacturing supervision, materials management, operations, packaging, product/service development, purchasing/procurement, quality, receiving, strategic sourcing, transportation/traffic/shipping and warehousing (ISM 2012). The various methods and approaches to continuous improvement are:

1) Benchmarking systems

Benchmarking as defined in the ISM *Glossary* (2014) is the process by which selected practices and results of one organization are compared to those of one or more other organizations to establish targets for improvement. Benchmarking can be performed by identifying world-class organizations and visiting them for information gathering and comparison, or by responding to surveys from third-party independent research organizations that collect, aggregate and disseminate benchmark data. A time line should be developed with set milestones and a target date for completion to keep the benchmarking project on track. Supply management professionals should also hold regularly scheduled meetings to assess the progress being made, and determine whether any corrective action is needed. Once the data has been collected, it will be collated and analyzed to determine long-term solutions for improvement (Yuva et al. 2001). The solution is then implemented and progress monitored. Benchmarks may need to be recalibrated as necessary.

2) Process mapping and value stream mapping

Process mapping is a method of drawing a pictorial representation of a process (for example, manufacturing a component or ordering a part) that breaks the process into key activities, transfers, decisions and approvals. Process maps enable analysis of the inputs, outputs and inter-relationships of each process to understand how processes interact in a system, locate process flaws that are creating systemic problems, evaluate which activities add value for the customer, mobilize teams to streamline and improve processes, and identify processes that need to be reengineered. Other commonly used terms are flow charting, flow diagrams, process diagrams and workflow diagrams (ISM *Glossary* 2014). The benefits of process mapping include ensuring a common understanding of the activities, results and the users involved in the specific business process. In addition, the use of process maps helps to define the boundaries of the business process and also develops a baseline of the business process which can then be used to measure the results of any business process improvement initiatives (Bozarth and Handfield 2012). A process map identifies the specific activities that make up the flow of the business process. This technique uses simple symbols, lines and words to graphically display the activities and sequence in the process (Harrington 1991). Some of the more common process mapping or flow charting symbols are illustrated below:

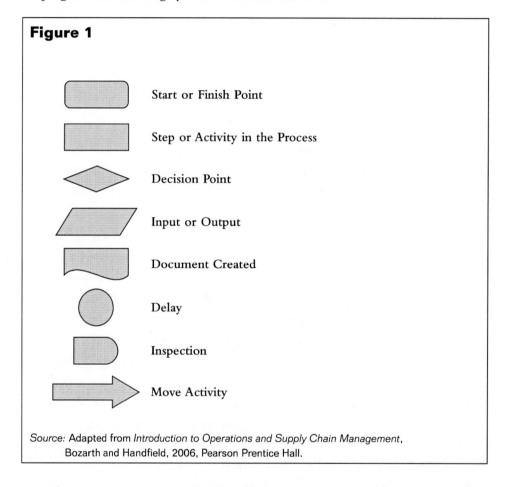

Figure 1

	Start or Finish Point
	Step or Activity in the Process
	Decision Point
	Input or Output
	Document Created
	Delay
	Inspection
	Move Activity

Source: Adapted from *Introduction to Operations and Supply Chain Management*, Bozarth and Handfield, 2006, Pearson Prentice Hall.

Value stream mapping (VSM) is a lean manufacturing technique in which the transformation of materials is traced from beginning to end to determine if there is waste in the process in the form of a step where no value is added or a point of "wait time" when material is being stored to await further value-adding transformation. This concept may also be applied to services (ISM *Glossary* 2014). VSM is similar to process mapping in that they both graphically describe the activities that constitute a process. VSM is focused on a broader view of the process, however, than traditional process mapping. VSM reflects the process from external supplier to external customer, and may even extend to tier-two and tier-three suppliers and distributors in the organization's supply chain. VSM is appropriate for high production, low variety product mixes with few components and subassemblies and dedicated equipment (Lee 2006).

3) Process costing

Process costing is an accounting method used for determining unit product costs in industries that produce homogenous products on a continuous basis or by using assembly operations. In process costing, material, labor and overhead costs are assigned to products for computing unit costs. Additionally, process costing accumulates costs by department as opposed to job orders, and assigns these costs uniformly to all units passing through that department (Garrison, Noreen and Brewer 2011).

Process costing, as used in process management and process improvement, is focused on determining the total cost of an organizational process to analyze the cost of the process and find ways to reduce them (Harrington 1991). Additionally, with process costing the total cost can be determined and then the cost of activities that are purely value-added can be computed, resulting in a value-add ratio which is the total value-add activity cost divided by the total process cost. A high value-add ratio reflects an efficient process, whereas a low value-add ratio reflects an inefficient process. Using the value-add ratio, processes can be analyzed to analyze the value-add activities and the non-value-add activities (Warren, Reeve and Duchac 2012).

4) Maturity models

The use of formal methods for measuring and assessing organizational effectiveness originated from the quality initiatives such as The Deming Prize, ISO standards and the Malcolm Baldrige National Quality Award. A maturity model is a methodology used to examine the different stages and requirements of projects, software or products to enable moving to the next step or level (ISM *Glossary* 2014). Maturity, in this sense, is defined as a measure of effectiveness in any specific process (Dinsmore 1998).

Some of the more recent developments in maturity models developed for measuring and assessing specific process capability and maturity have been developed in the areas of software development, project management and contract management.

A) **Capability maturity model integration (CMMI)**

The capability maturity model integration developed by the Software Engineering Institute (SEI) is a process improvement approach that provides organizations with the essential elements of effective processes. It can be used to guide process improvement across a project, a division or an entire organization. CMMI helps integrate traditionally separate organizational functions, set process improvement goals and priorities, provide guidance for quality processes and provide a point of reference for appraising current processes (SEI 2006).

The CMMI covers the following areas of interest: acquisition, development and services. Based on practices that describe the characteristic of effective processes, the CMMI is used as a guide for improvement of project and organizational processes, and includes an appraisal method to diagnose the state of an organization's current practices. The CMMI contains five maturity levels: initial, managed, defined, quantitatively managed and optimizing (SEI 2006).

B) **Contract management maturity model (CMMM)**

The contract management maturity model is a roadmap developed by an organization to help it assess, measure and improve its contract management processes and relationships, including roles and responsibilities, timelines, performance management and costs. The model measures the effectiveness of an organization's contract management processes and helps it identify the level of maturity: ad hoc, basic, structured, integrated or optimized (ISM *Glossary* 2014). The ad hoc level (Level 1) indicates no formal contracting structure is in place; basic (Level 2) means an organization has a basic, disciplined process capability; structured (Level 3) designates the contracting organization is fully established and has institutionalized processes capability; integrated (Level 4) suggests that contract management processes are integrated with other corporate processes resulting in synergistic corporate benefits; and optimized (Level 5) means the organization has processes focused on continuous improvement and adoption of lessons learned and best practices (Garrett and Rendon 2005).

The CMMM creates a vision of excellence to help buying and selling organizations focus on the key areas of process improvement. It provides its users with a framework or a guide for improving their respective levels of performance. It is envisioned that the model and survey assessment tool will serve as the foundation for ongoing discussion and further development within the contract management profession.

The CMMM provides a visual tool to help an organization assess the major steps which they must accomplish when either buying or selling products, services or integrated solutions, in both public and private business sectors. The maturity levels reflected in the model allow an organization to assess their level of capability for each of the six major steps, in their respective buying or selling processes. The contract management process for the supply management professional includes procurement planning, solicitation planning, solicitation, source selection, contract administration and contract closeout (Garrett and Rendon 2005).

5) Process improvement metrics

Process management is the function of planning, organizing, controlling and improving a process and measuring its utility in providing the desired end result (ISM *Glossary* 2014). It also includes measuring performance. The most common process improvement metrics include productivity, efficiency and cycle time.

Productivity is a measure of the ratio of outputs to inputs. Using monetary units or some other unit of measure, higher productivity reflects increased outputs and decreased inputs (Bozarth and Handfield 2012).

Efficiency is a measure of actual outputs compared to a standard output measure. This standard output measure is an estimate of what should be produced, given a certain level of resources. A 100 percent efficiency reflects a process that is producing at the most efficient level. Efficiency levels below 100 percent reflect less efficient processes (Bozarth and Handfield 2012).

Cycle time is a measure of the total elapsed time needed to complete the process. The use of cycle time as a process improvement metric has some advantages, including that when cycle time is reduced, there is typically an increase in performance in other areas such as quality, delivery, productivity and efficiency (Bozarth and Handfield 2012).

6) Process improvement methods (for example, lean methods, JIT, lean six sigma, value stream mapping)

Process improvement methods include the various tools and techniques used to improve the various business processes of an organization. Some of the more common process improvement methods include just in time (JIT), lean production and lean six sigma.

JIT is a system in which materials are purchased, transported and processed "just in time" for their use in a subsequent stage of the manufacturing process. It is an operations management philosophy whose objectives are to reduce waste and cycle time. Operationally, JIT minimizes inventory at all levels. It requires consistent quality at the appropriate level and frequent on-time delivery of small lot sizes (ISM *Glossary* 2014). The objectives of JIT are to have only the required inventory when needed; to have zero defects; to reduce lead times through reductions in setup times, queue lengths, and lot sizes; and to accomplish all of this at minimum cost (Bozarth and Handfield 2012).

Lean production is a philosophy of operation that focuses on minimization of all resources (including time) used in the enterprise. It employs a set of principles and practices to reduce cost through the relentless removal of waste and through the simplification of all processes (ISM *Glossary* 2014).

Lean six sigma is a combination of six sigma quality with lean production to eliminate waste and achieve major cost, inventory and lead time reductions in less than a year (ISM *Glossary* 2014). Six sigma is a systematic methodology developed by Motorola that uses information and service-related processes to reduce defects in products and services. The philosophy behind six sigma is that, by measuring how many defects are in a process, an organization may identify how to systematically eliminate the defects to get as close to perfection as possible. As a metric, six sigma equates to 3.4 defects per one million opportunities (DPMO) (ISM *Glossary* 2014).

Value stream mapping (VSM), another process improvement technique, is described in Item 2 of Task 2-G-2. The steps to making improvements are: (1) identify a target product, product family or service; (2) draw a value stream map of the current state of the production process including the current steps, any delays, and required information flows required to deliver the product or service; (3) assess the current state of the value stream map and determine how current flows can be improved to eliminate waste; (4) draw the future state value stream map based on the assessment; and (5) work toward adopting the future state condition (Rother and Shook 2014).

7) Supplier workshops

Supplier workshops can be another source of process improvement, specifically as it relates to the buying organization's supply chain. In supplier workshops, the buying organization and its critical suppliers collaborate on process improvement opportunities that will result in a more streamlined supply chain and thus benefit all supply chain partners (Burt, Dobler and Starling 2003).

BIBLIOGRAPHY

Bozarth, C.C. and R.B. Handfield. *Introduction to Operations and Supply Chain Management*, Pearson Prentice-Hall, Upper Saddle River, NJ, 2012.

Burt, D.N., D.W. Dobler and S.L. Starling. *World Class Supply Management*, McGraw-Hill Irwin, New York, 2003.

Cavinato, J.L., A.E. Flynn, M.L. Harding, C.S. Lallatin, M.L. Peck, H.M. Pohlig, S.R. Sturzl and V. Tucker (Eds.). ISM *Glossary of Key Supply Management Terms*, 6th edition, Institute for Supply Management®, Tempe, AZ, 2014.

CMMI® for Acquisition, Version 1.3, Carnegie Mellon, November 2010, http://www.sei.cmu.edu/library/abstracts/reports/10tr032.cfm, accessed June 27, 2013.

Curtis, B., W.E. Hefley and S.A. Miller. *People Capability Maturity Model*, Addison-Wesley, 2001.

Dinsmore, P.C. *Winning in Business with Enterprise Project Management*, AMACOM, 1998.

Garrett, G.A. and R.G. Rendon. *Contract Management: Organizational Assessment Tools*, National Contract Management Association, Ashburn, VA, 2005.

Garrison, R.H., E.W. Noreen and P.C. Brewer. *Managerial Accounting for Managers, 3rd Edition*, McGraw-Hill Irwin, New York, 2014.

Harrington, H.J. *Business Process Improvement*, McGraw-Hill and ASQC Quality Press, 1991.

Harrington, H.J. *The Improvement Process*, McGraw-Hill and ASQC Quality Press, 1987.

Lee, Q. T*he Strategos Guide to Value Stream Mapping & Process Mapping*, Strategos, Inc., accessed from http://www.strategosinc.com/vsm_mapping_guide.htm, 2006.

Rother, M. and J. Shook, *Learning to See*, Lean Enterprise Institute, 2014.

Warren, C.S., Reeve, J.E. and J.E. Duchac. *Financial and Managerial Accounting, 11th edition*, South-Western/Cengage Learning, 2012.

Yuva, J., T. Dolan, K. Killen, C. Rasborn, R. Tevelson and D.S. Wade (2001). "Benchmarking for the Future," *Purchasing Today*, Vol. 12 (1), p. 40.

Quality

Task 2–H–1

Develop and administer a supplier certification program.

Supplier certification is an organization's process for evaluating the quality systems of key suppliers in an effort to eliminate incoming inspections (ISM *Glossary* 2014).

1) Supplier quality practices

Supply management departments sometimes categorize suppliers (according to certain criteria) as "preferred," "partnered," "certified" and "prequalified." These categorizations generally indicate that the organization has evaluated the suppliers as possessing the quality and operating systems that meet customer needs. In the evaluation process, supply management professionals may evaluate not only their primary suppliers but also second- or third-tier suppliers that support their primary suppliers. This type of evaluation gives the supply management organization a higher level of confidence in its primary suppliers' capabilities.

Supply management professionals with established lists of recommended suppliers will also have a process to recognize supplier performance over a period of time. When a supplier's performance remains high over a period of time, it achieves a higher level of recognition by the supply management organization. As the supplier achieves each level of performance, a higher level of trust, improved integration into the supply management organization and an increased use of quality systems or statistical process control (SPC) to monitor performance results are achieved. Supply management organizations may categorize suppliers to meet specific needs as follows:

- Approved suppliers — Suppliers that meet an organization's selection criteria and have been added to the approved list (ISM *Glossary* 2014). The approval process may include submission of samples for testing or other steps to approve the item or service to be purchased. It may also include inspection of the supplier's quality systems.

- Preferred suppliers — A group of suppliers that an organization has determined meet its expectations for quality, delivery and/or price and that are able to respond to unexpected changes. Often the organization establishes master price agreements with preferred suppliers. For items where preferred suppliers have been identified, the entire organization is required to buy from these suppliers (ISM *Glossary* 2014).

- Partnered suppliers — The term "partnership" or "partnered supplier" refers to a close relationship between a buyer and seller to attain some advantages from each other in a positive way. A partnership in this context does not imply a legal relationship. Buyer-seller partnerships may be of operational importance, such as a long-term, single-source relationship with an office supplier, or of strategic importance, such as a long-term, single-source relationship with a supplier of a good or service of strategic importance (ISM *Glossary* 2014). Such relationships are usually built around long-term arrangements, large volume commitments, and joint product or service process development. Electronic links between the organizations may automate ordering and delivery scheduling. Such arrangements generally work best when there is a mutual benefit in forming a relationship (for example, to compete with another set of organizations for the same customers). Many organizations are moving away from using the word "partner" because of its specific legal meaning. In many organizations, terms such as "strategic alliance" and "special relationship" are used to indicate a supplier association that is based on more than the traditional price-based, arm's length model.

- Certified suppliers — A certified supplier is one whose quality control system has proven to be highly reliable, thus eliminating the need for incoming inspection (ISM *Glossary* 2014). This supplier is integrated with the supply management professional's enterprisewide quality control system, and through which a larger quality assurance system is established. In this way, total costs associated with quality are reduced through the elimination of duplicate efforts, and use of SPC and other quality control processes and information sources. The supply management organization typically defines the standards that suppliers must meet to become certified. In some industries, there are also standards agreed upon by the entire industry.

- Prequalified suppliers — Prequalified or approved suppliers are suppliers that meet an organization's selection criteria and have been added to the approved list (ISM *Glossary* 2014) This consists of closely examining the suppliers to determine such factors as financial strength, facilities, location, size, technology, labor status, management, costs, terms, references and other factors. Such suppliers are therefore prequalified to do business with the organization.

- Certifiable suppliers — A certifiable supplier is one that is not currently certified by the supply management organization but is in the process of becoming certified, may already be certified by another division of the same organization or may be certified by another organization.

- Disqualified suppliers — Individuals or organizations that fail to meet the standards established by a supply management organization and are barred from competing for that organization's business (ISM *Glossary* 2014). Typically, a supplier would not be disqualified until several steps had been taken to attempt to correct the underlying performance problems. Disqualifying a supplier is a last resort.

- Acceptance testing — These are test procedures that lead to formal acceptance of a new or changed product, process or system. For example, the overall condition of a given lot may be determined by inspecting only a portion or sample of the lot. For a software system, a user acceptance test plan is agreed to by the buyer and seller, carried out, and results are compared to pre-established severity thresholds to determine corrective action (ISM *Glossary* 2014).

- Certification requirements — Organizations may create quality standards that, when achieved, become the basis for the supplier to be certified, thereby qualifying for reduction or elimination of incoming inspections. These standards usually include definitions of how the measurements are made and the minimum level of quality that will no longer require inspection. To become certified, suppliers review their measurement system with the supply management organization to ensure that the measurements are correlated and to provide documentation that the minimum certifiable quality levels have been achieved.

Under the Uniform Commercial Code (UCC), after a reasonable opportunity to inspect the goods, supply management professionals become responsible for all defects that incoming inspections should have uncovered, even if no inspection took place. Documenting the certification arrangements with suppliers (and defining the liability for quality problems discovered later) can avert potential issues. Supply management professionals should make sure that both parties sign the documented agreement.

Inspections may occur at many places and may have many levels of thoroughness. The locations of inspections may include:

- The supplier's plant, in process, as goods are made or as a service is performed

- The supplier's plant, at inspection stations

- The supplier's plant, at final inspection before shipment or at the end of a service

- The supply management professional's organization, at incoming inspection

- The supply management professional's organization, in process, as the supplier's materials are used

- The supply management professional's organization, at final inspection before shipment.

The earlier inspections occur, the more likely the problems and service issues will be corrected. Suppliers that use process controls and inspect as materials are made (and that correct problems immediately) are least likely to ship a defective product.

The levels of thoroughness of inspections include:

- No inspections at all

- Occasional audits or random inspections (for example, for certified suppliers)

- Routine sample inspections

- One hundred percent inspections (such as automated testing).

Thoroughness early in the process can eliminate or drastically reduce service problems or the need for inspections later in the process.

The results of inspections (anywhere in the process) should be documented in a format that is easily understandable by both the supply management professional and the seller. If inspections take place at the supply management professional's facility, then the data will become the basis of the supplier's quality measurement and should be provided to the supplier on a regular basis. If inspections take place at the supplier's facility, the supplier can provide that data to the supply management professional as proof of quality.

2) Supplier certifications/registrations (for example, ISO or Good Manufacturing Practices [GMP])

Customers may require that their suppliers seek and maintain ISO 9000:2005 registration or other types of registrations or certifications. ISO 9000:2005 and ISO/TS 16949 are discussed below. ISO 9000:2005 is perhaps the most common supplier registration standard used worldwide. ISO/TS 16949 is a standard created for a specific industry (automotive) and is simply provided as an example that is well known.

ISO 9000:2005 basics — ISO 9000 is not a prescription for running a business or an organization. However, its requirements provide a recognized international quality standard that businesses can follow. To effectively use the ISO standard, processes need to be planned and followed. The organization must correct deficiencies in current processes and strive to continually improve.

The original version of ISO 9000 was implemented internationally in 1994 by the International Organization for Standardization (ISO) Technical Committee. ISO 9000:2005 is a much simplified document.

The standards are:

1) ISO 9000:2005 — Quality management systems – Fundamentals and vocabulary.

2) ISO 9001:2008 — Quality management systems – Requirements. This specifies the requirements of a quality management system. These are used for internal implementation, contractual purposes or third-party registrations.

3) ISO 9004:2009 — Quality management – Guidelines for performance improvement. This broader document provides guidelines for objectives that are not included in ISO 9001:2000. These include continual improvement and enhancing overall performance.

4) ISO 19011:2012 — provides guidelines for internal and external audits of quality and/or environmental management systems.

ISO 9001:2008 consists of five sections:

- Clause 4: Quality Management System Requirements

- Clause 5: Management's Responsibility

- Clause 6: Resource Management

- Clause 7: Product Realization

- Clause 8: Measurement, Monitoring Analysis and Improvement.

For more information about ISO 9000:2005, contact the International Organization for Standardization in Geneva, Switzerland, at www.iso.org.

The following eight principles provide the foundation for ISO 9000:2005. These are mentioned in ISO 9000 and 9004, but not in ISO 9001. They are:

1) Customer focus

2) Leadership

3) Involvement of people

4) The process approach

5) A systems approach to management

6) Continual improvement

7) Factual approach to decision-making

8) Mutually beneficial supplier relationships.

The ISO registration process typically takes several months from initial meeting to final registration audit. This time frame differs from client to client, but each process usually follows the steps below.

Step 1 — Inquiry where the organization contacts registrars to investigate the terms for registration. The prospective organization then makes a final selection of a registrar with whom the organization is comfortable.

Step 2 — The organization contracts with the registrar. In this process, registration steps are determined and a price is negotiated. A signed quotation or purchase order leads to the first stage of the certification process. Some organizations may wish to have a pre-assessment or gap analysis audit.

Step 3 — Often involves a phase 1 audit. At this stage, the registrar performs an on-site audit of the documented quality system against the applicable standard.

Step 4 — The certification audit. Every element of the ISO 9000 standard is audited several times during the registration process. Representative samples of an organization's business processes are chosen for any audit. During each three-year period, 100 percent of the organization is audited. The audit program is a valuable tool that provides a clearly and mutually defined process and snapshot of auditing — past, present and future.

Step 5 — May involve process audits (optional). The organization may choose business processes for auditing to the applicable standard, allowing the client to learn and experience the registrar's auditing methods and style.

Step 6 — Involves the final certification audit. Once the organization's documented quality system has met the applicable standard, the registrar will conduct an audit to determine the system's effective implementation. This may involve interviewing the process owners and responsible personnel as designated in the documented quality system for processes chosen from the audit program.

Step 7 — After certification; involves rolling certification audits. These are sometimes referred to as surveillance audits where the registrar returns on either six-month or annual cycles.

ISO/TS 16949:2009 — The ISO/TS 16949 was jointly developed by members and of the International Automotive Task Force (IAFT) submitted to ISO for approval and publication. The document is a common automotive quality system requirements catalog based on ISO 9001:2008 and specific requirements from the automotive sector. This document, coupled with customer-specific requirements, defines quality system requirements for use in the automotive supply chain.

IATF members include the following vehicle manufacturers: BMW Group, Chrysler Group, Daimler AG, Fiat Group Automobile, Ford Motor Company, General Motors Company, PSA Peugeot Citroen, Renault SA, Volkswagen AG and the vehicle manufacturers' respective trade associations — AIAG (U.S.), ANFIA (Italy), FIEV (France), SMMT (U.K.) and VDA (Germany).

Best management practices (BMPs) and good manufacturing practices (GMPs) are generally practices that are encouraged or required by regulatory agencies. For example, the U.S. Food and Drug Administration (FDA) publish BMPs for food manufacturers. Medical instrument manufacturers follow FDA GMPs. Some of these require the use of lean manufacturing or SPC.

3) Congruence of test methodologies and results between buying and selling organizations

Many times an organization will want to work with its suppliers to achieve consistency in quality practices. This will include the following areas:

- Acceptance/rejection history — What do the records indicate about the supplier's performance? Acceptance or rejection history should be readily available and reviewed, along with traceable records. A check should be made to ensure that measuring device calibration dates have not expired.

- Testing capability — What abilities does the organization have to detect correct and incorrect work by both the workers and equipment? A batch sampling technique or some form of statistical sampling procedure will most likely be used instead of 100 percent inspection of the incoming components. Final examination of the finished product will probably take place in a secured area awaiting final release. Quality control personnel should do the examination, and the inspection procedures should be in writing. Test methods, procedures and instruments should be the same as those used by the supply management professional's incoming quality control procedures to ensure compatibility. All gauges and test devices should be reviewed to ensure that calibration dates are current. Shop floor quality checks should be conducted at regular intervals to verify those performed during the process by production floor employees.

- Workers — Indicators of worker capability to look for might include the number of hours of statistical quality control (SQC) or total quality management (TQM) training, worker certifications held, and the use of process control charts by the equipment operators.

- Machines — The equipment capability can be monitored in several ways. The supply management professional can look at the maintenance history of key elements in the process for frequency of breakdowns and preventive maintenance activity. The presence of process control charts is another way to monitor machine capability.

- Process control — What types of quality detection and correction systems are used? Primary systems in effect today include statistical process control (SPC) and six sigma/Cpk. Validation of the manufacturing process should be properly documented. If the organization has a program of statistical quality control or statistical process control (SQC/SPC) in place, it should be reviewed.

  Statistical process control (SPC)/statistical quality control (SQC) — SPC/SQC involves checking products while they are being produced. Samples are periodically taken by line employees and compared to the range of existing tolerance. If a product is out of its tolerance range, it is stopped and corrected. This ensures that no additional out-of-tolerance products are produced. There should be control charts at individual workstations indicating that checks are being made during production.

  Six sigma/Cpk process bounds — Six sigma is a quality management program with a goal of no more than three defects per million parts and an outstanding commitment to quality. Cpk refers to a quality measurement index for process capability. This helps to determine whether or not products consistently meet their specifications.

  Organization and management of quality systems — What are the overall organizational systems in place for quality? Is it the traditional "check after an item was made," or is it a proactive system that checks the work as it is being produced?

  Documented systems/procedures — All inspection procedures should be in writing, and a solid training program with periodic updates should be in place.

  System certification/validation — Supply management professionals today are requiring various types of quality certification of suppliers.

These range from being qualified, to being certified, to complete quality assurance. Many forms and distinctions are in use.

4) Organizational requirements for supplier certification (for example, evidence of statistical process control [SPC])

Some of the organizational requirements relative to ISO 9000:2005 and ISO/TS 16949 have been addressed. The following are some additional areas that organizations have examined to certify a supplier. These may vary on an industry-by-industry and organization-by-organization basis.

Management responsibility — Supplier management is responsible for defining and documenting its policies for quality along with its objectives and its level of commitment. Hence, quality policy must be documented and implemented at all levels within the organization.

Quality system — A supplier must have a defined and documented system for defining how quality objectives will be met. This includes a process for planning quality improvement.

Contract review — Contract review involves the steps associated with contracting with suppliers. This includes acceptance of the contract or order, the tender of a contract and review of the contract. Contract requirements must be adequately documented. Records of contract reviews are maintained and procedures associated with contracts are documented.

Design control — For those suppliers that design products, design controls focus on designing processes. To meet the requirements of the design control standard, suppliers establish and maintain procedures for controlling the design of the product. Among the areas that are addressed in design control are design and development planning. For example, suppliers to major automotive organizations must be qualified in skills such as value engineering, geometric tolerancing and dimensioning, the Taguchi method and other approaches to design engineering.

Document and data control — Document and data control includes the procedures or approvals in issuing documents and data and making changes to such data. Examples of documents that are considered for document and data control include engineering drawings, engineering standards, inspection instructions, test procedures and other documented processes.

Procurement — To satisfy requirements for procurement, the supplier must establish and maintain documents of procedures to ensure that purchased products conform to specified standards. Procedures must be in place for developing subcontractors and scheduling production among subcontractors. Procurement documents must contain data clearly describing the product ordered, including product characteristics for the item being purchased.

Control of customer-supplied product — In some circumstances, customers supply products to suppliers. At times, these are used in the production of components for the final products. The standard for this element is worded as follows: "Suppliers must establish and maintain documented procedures for the control of verification, storage and maintenance of customer-supplied product provided for incorporation into supplies or for related activities."

Product identification and traceability — Requirements for product traceability differ from industry to industry but often the ability to trace product components is important for legal, regulatory or liability reasons. An example is beef for determining the origin of mad cow disease or to verify that it is truly beef and not some other form of meat.

Process control —The element relating to process control establishes that suppliers identify and plan the production, installation and servicing processes that result in quality products. One condition is documented procedures defining the means of production, installation and servicing as well as how the lack of such procedures could adversely affect quality. Another condition is the use of suitable production, installation and servicing equipment as well as a suitable working environment. Process control documents demonstrate how the organization conforms to all government safety and environmental regulations. This includes compliance with codes and standards, quality plans and procedures.

Inspection and testing — To ensure that processes are functioning properly, inspection testing activities are put in place to ensure that specified requirements for products are met. This includes any acceptance sampling criteria that are established and procedures for using accredited laboratory facilities to provide external validation. This procedure includes requirements for receiving inspection and testing to ensure incoming product quality. Other aspects of inspection and testing that must be documented are in-process inspection testing and final inspection testing using statistical process control (SPC). Also, inspection and test records must be established and maintained to provide evidence that products have been inspected and tested.

Control of inspection, measuring and test equipment — So that inspections are accurate, measurement and testing equipment must be kept in top condition. For this to occur, suppliers must establish and maintain document procedures to control, calibrate and maintain inspection, measuring and test equipment — including test software used by the supplier.

Inspection and test status — Relating to inspection measuring that has been discussed, another aspect of inspection is maintaining current inspection and test status. This ensures that all products have passed required inspection and testing.

Control of nonconforming product — When nonconforming products are produced, four things can happen:

- They can be reworked to meet specified requirements.

- They can be accepted with or without repair or concessions.

- They can be re-graded for alternative applications.

- They can be rejected and scrapped.

Corrective and preventive action — When problems occur with processes resulting in defective products for improving processes, a standard process for addressing problems is needed so that corrective and preventive action can take place. Suppliers must use a disciplined approach to solving problems when errors occur in a process.

Handling, storage, packaging, preservation and delivery — This has to do with the supply management issues of logistics and inventory control. Among the areas to be documented are inventory control methods such as models, how inventory turnovers are optimized and how inventory levels are minimized. This might include a discussion of just in time (JIT) methods used by the supplier. In addition, packaging standards are documented and labeling standards are discussed. If relevant, stock preservation methods are documented. Finally, supplier delivery performance monitoring, production scheduling and shipment notification systems are documented.

Control of quality records — This standard states that the supplier must establish and hold documented procedures for identifying, collecting, indexing, accessing, filing, storing, maintaining and disposing of quality related records. The purpose of quality records is to show whether the quality system is achieving its intended goals of ensuring quality.

Internal quality audits — These are prioritized in relation to the importance of the various quality related functions that occur in the process. Individuals who do not have line authority in the organization must perform these audits. Follow-up audits verify that corrective action has taken place to address inadequacies in the quality delivery system.

Training — A supplier organization must have documented procedures for assessing training needs and for training all personnel who affect an organization's quality. Records of past training must also be kept.

Servicing — Interestingly, the verbiage for the servicing section is rather short. Basically, it states that servicing should meet the customer's specified requirements. In addition, a method for communicating about service must be maintained.

Statistical techniques — Appropriate statistical techniques are chosen during advanced quality planning and are to be kept in the control plan.

BIBLIOGRAPHY

Cavinato, J.L., A.E. Flynn, M.L. Harding, C.S. Lallatin, M.L. Peck, H.M. Pohlig, S.R. Sturzl and V. Tucker (Eds.). ISM *Glossary of Key Supply Management Terms*, 6th edition, Institute for Supply Management®, Tempe, AZ, 2014.

Foster, S.T. Jr. *Managing Quality: Integrating the Supply Chain*, 5/E, Prentice Hall, Upper Saddle River, NJ, 2013.

International Automotive Task Force (IATF), ISO/TS 16949, http://www.iatfglobaloversight.org/, accessed July 20, 2013.

Monczka, R.M., Handfield, R.B., Giunipero, L.C. and J.L. Patterson. *Purchasing and Supply Chain Management*, South-Western Cengage Learning, 2011.

ISO, Selection and Use of the ISO 9000 Family Standards, 2009, http://www.iso.org/iso/iso_9000_selection_and_use-2009.pdf.

Task 2–H–2
Develop measurements for continuous quality improvement and target setting.

Organizations should continuously seek improvements in quality to increase their competitive advantage. Quality improvements are the enhancements that increase value or decrease the time requirements of processes, activities, performance, products and other areas (ISM *Glossary* 2014). Attaining these improvements requires a systematic approach based on predetermined targets and includes quality control activities, quality assurance processes and quality management programs.

1) Quality control

A) **Definition** — Quality control involves measuring quality performance and comparing it with specification requirements as a basis for controlling output quality levels. The quality assurance function is responsible for this activity (ISM *Glossary* 2014).

2) Quality assurance

A) **Definition** — Quality assurance is a management function that includes establishing specifications that can be met by suppliers; utilizing suppliers that have the capability to provide adequate quality within those specifications; applying control processes that assure high-quality products and services; and developing the means for measuring the product, service and cost performance of suppliers and comparing it with requirements (ISM *Glossary* 2014).

B) **Acceptance testing** — Acceptance testing is defined in the ISM *Glossary* (2014) as test procedures that lead to formal acceptance of a new or changed product, process or system. For example, the overall condition of a given lot may be determined by inspecting only a portion or sample of the lot. For a software system, a user acceptance test plan is agreed to by the buyer and seller, carried out and results are compared to pre-established severity thresholds to determine corrective action.

There are times when the receiving organization must inspect incoming materials from its suppliers. At these times, acceptance sampling is the technique that is used. When materials are received, the organization can use a range of alternatives, from 100 percent inspection to inspecting a relative few and drawing inferences about the entire shipment.

Is acceptance sampling needed? Acceptance sampling has been controversial. Some disagree with acceptance sampling because they are fundamentally opposed to the notion of an acceptable level of defects that is greater than zero. Also, many feel the notion of the acceptable quality level (AQL) is counter to Deming's concepts of continual improvement. However, there is still a need for acceptance sampling in many different circumstances. Following are times when acceptance sampling might be needed:

- When dealing with new or unproven suppliers

- During start-ups and when building new products

- When product can be damaged in shipment

- With extremely sensitive products

- When product can spoil during shipment (such as agricultural seed)

- When problems with a certain supplier that have been noticed in the production process bring the supplier's performance into question.

Acceptance sampling is a statistical quality control technique used in deciding to accept or reject a shipment of input or output. When compared with statistical quality control, acceptance sampling is defined by its occurrence after production has been completed. This can be either at the beginning of the process when receiving components, parts or raw materials from a supplier or at the end of production as in the case of final inspection. The focus will be on inspection of incoming materials.

Producer's and consumer's risk — Producer's risk is the risk associated with rejecting a lot of materials that has good quality. For example, a producer of a product that has high quality has a customer that has concluded that the product has poor quality and returns the product. In this case, the producer has been judged inaccurately. Consumer's risk is the exact opposite. As a consumer, a shipment of a poor quality product has been received and the product has good quality. Therefore, the consumer pays for the product, uses it in the production process and suffers the consequences. Producer's risk is denoted by alpha (β) and consumer's risk is denoted by beta (α). The goal of acceptance sampling is to reduce producer's risk to low levels while maintaining consumer's risk at acceptable levels.

The acceptable quality level (AQL) represents the process limit of a measured attribute averaged from a series of satisfactory lots. AQL is typically used for sample inspection (ISM *Glossary* 2014). This concept of the acceptable quality level has been troublesome to many who consider this an acceptance of less-than-perfect quality. To statisticians this is simply an economic decision that is associated with producer's risk.

Lot tolerance percent defective (LTPD) is the level of poor quality that is included in a lot of goods. The differences between AQL and LTPD are sometimes confusing. Lots of AQL or better should usually have an alpha (that is, for example, a 5 percent) or less chance of rejection. This is related to Type I error. Lots of LTPD or worse should have a beta (that is, say, a 10 percent) or less chance of acceptance. This relates to Type II error. There is theoretically only one combination of sample size (n) and acceptance number (c) that meets both conditions simultaneously. In practice, both conditions would be unable to be met precisely, and the supply management professional must choose a combination of n and c that approximates both conditions simultaneously. The selection of the sample size n and the acceptance number c is referred to as the sampling plan.

For the most part, the assignment of AQL, LTPD, alpha (α) and beta (β) is a management decision. Once these values are determined, values for n and c can be determined. The bottom line in acceptance sampling is that acceptance sampling plans are designed to give two things, n and c, in which:

n = the sample size of a particular sampling plan, and

c = the maximum number of defective pieces for a sample to be rejected.

The average sampling plan can be stated in simple terms; that is, n = 20 and c = 5. This clearly communicates the bounds of the sampling plan: take a sample of 20 items and if five are defective, reject the lot of materials. It is important to remember that the supply management professional should always randomize when selecting product from a supplier to be inspected.

Types of samples — The discussion has focused on sampling plans for single samples. This is not the limit of sampling plans. More complex sampling plans are referred to as multiple sampling plans or sequential sampling plans. With these sampling plans, the acceptance sampling rules might occur as follows:

n_1 = sample size for sample # 1

n_2 = sample size for sample # 2

n_n = sample size for sample # n

c_1 = acceptance number for sample # 1

c_2 = acceptance number for sample # 2

c_n = acceptance number for sample # n

r_1 = rejection number for sample # 1

r_2 = rejection number for sample # 2

r_n = rejection number for sample # n

Multiple sampling plans have advantages over single sampling plans. The sample size used in multiple sampling plans will have a smaller average sample size with the same amount of protection as a single sampling plan. The decision relating to multiple sampling plans will usually be made on the first phase of the sample. This then results in smaller samples.

Acceptance sampling in continuous production — The single and double sampling plans are called lot-by-lot sampling plans. As separate samples are performed, additional lots of materials are received. Sometimes it is not feasible to collect products into lots as they are produced in a continuous manner. In these cases, acceptance sampling procedures for continuous production are used. These procedures typically involve alternating between 100 percent inspection and sampling inspection.

C) **Certification requirements** — See Task 2–H–1 for information on certification requirements.

D) **Quality documentation** — Typically, documentation requirements are specified by either the customer or the registrar. These may vary. Many of the requirements were outlined in Task 2–H–1. However, this simply requires developing standard operations procedures according to the customer's or registrar's requirements.

E) **"Best-in-class" benchmarks** — A benchmark is a standard or point of reference used in measuring or judging an organization's performance according to selected criteria (ISM *Glossary* 2014). A benchmark is an organization that is recognized for its exemplary operational performance. A benchmark is not an average; it is the best.

Since benchmarks are outstanding organizations, benchmarking means to document performance and compare that performance to that of the best organizations. To facilitate the discussion, the terms "initiator organization" and "target organization" will be used. The initiator organization is the organization that initiates contact and studies another organization. The target organization is the organization that is being studied (also called a benchmarking partner). These are not static roles as the target organization often enters into a reciprocal agreement to observe the initiator organization. Besides providing inputs to improvement, benchmarking is useful for externally validating an organization's approach to its business. Several types of benchmarking are found in the quality literature and are defined below. Note they are not all mutually exclusive.

- Process benchmarking is a performance comparison of business processes against an internal or external standard of recognized leaders. Most often the comparison is made against a similar process in another organization considered to be best-in-class. This can involve studying process flows, operating systems, process technologies and the operations of target organizations or departments.

- Financial benchmarking usually involves using financial databases. The Internet is an important tool that can be searched for benchmarking financial performance.

- Performance benchmarking allows initiator organizations to assess competitive position by comparing products and services with target organizations. Performance issues may include cost structures, various types of productivity performance, speed of concept to market, quality measures and other performance evaluations.

- Product benchmarking is performed by many organizations when designing new products or upgrades to current products. This type of benchmarking often includes reverse engineering or dismantling competitors' products to understand the strengths and weaknesses of their designs.

- Strategic benchmarking involves the practice of observing how others compete. This is rarely industry specific as organizations go outside their own industries and learn lessons from organizations around the world. This typically involves target organizations that have been identified as world-class or high-performance such as Baldrige, Shingo or Deming prize winners.

- Functional benchmarking is another type of benchmarking. An example of functional benchmarking occurs in supply management. The Institute for Supply Management (ISM) provides a framework for the networking of supply management professionals. This allows for the functional sharing of information.

There are several primary purposes for benchmarking. These different purposes also imply differing levels of involvement in the benchmarking activities. How much time will need to be devoted to the project as well as costs involved may vary according to the purpose. The purposes of benchmarking range from just learning to becoming best-in-breed to achieving world-class leadership.

3) Quality management

A) **Definition** — Quality management is the function of planning, organizing, controlling and improving the quality of products and processes (ISM *Glossary* 2014). This involves leadership and prioritization of quality improvement activities in the organization.

B) **Meeting customer needs** — One of the important determinants of quality is how well an organization satisfies or delights its customers. Often customers are defined as internal or external customers. Internal customers are those within the organization receiving internal goods or services. In a sense, an economic transaction takes place in internal services in that service providers are funded as a result of the services they provide to the organization as a whole. Other authors have used an abstraction of the term "internal customer" to include the person at the next step in a process. Therefore, the person who works at workstation number 3 can be considered the customer of the worker at workstation number 2.

External customers are the bill-paying receivers of the work. The external customers are the ultimate people whom the organization is trying to satisfy with its products or services. If the organization has satisfied external customers, it will continue to prosper, grow and fulfill the objectives of the organization.

Another term that describes customers is "end user." An end user is someone who is at the end of the chain of events that results in the production of a product or service. Software developers who are programming software solutions for customers often use the term "end user." Service organizations have many titles for customers. These titles include patient, registrant, stockholder, buyer, patron and many others. As service and product producers, the customer is the focus of activities.

Often customer satisfaction surveys and focus groups are used to determine levels of customer satisfaction. Once these measures are in place, a baseline should be created and tracked over time to determine if improvement efforts have resulted in heightened levels of customer satisfaction.

C) **Quality tools** — In this section, the seven basic tools of quality, the seven managerial tools and various other tools will be defined. Kaoru Ishikawa, the inventor of the seven basic tools, was known for "democratizing statistics." What does this mean? Statistical concepts are difficult for many people to understand. For the average person, a means was needed to obtain the power of inferential statistics without the in-depth knowledge required to use parametric statistics correctly. Statisticians have long understood the importance of visual tools for communicating and understanding statistical concepts. Ishikawa adapted and invented these simple tools, known as the seven basic tools of quality (B7), so the average person could analyze and interpret data. These tools have been used in thousands of organizations and by all levels of managers and employees with worldwide success. While an in-depth discussion of these tools can be found elsewhere, the following provides a simple definition:

- Histograms — The first tool of quality is a histogram. It is a diagram of values being measured versus the frequency with which each occurs. When a process is running normally (only common causes are present), the histogram is depicted by a bell-shaped curve (ISM *Glossary* 2014).

- Pareto charts — Discussed in several areas of the Certified Professional in Supply Management® (CPSM®) exam specification, Pareto charts are graphs showing the frequency with which events occur, arranged in order of descending frequency. They are used to rank order the issues so that resources can be applied first to those with the largest potential return (ISM *Glossary* 2014). These are actually histograms that are aided by the 80/20 rule adapted by Joseph Juran from Vilfredo Pareto, the Italian economist. The 80/20 rule states that 80 percent of the problems are created by 20 percent of the causes. This means there are a few vital causes that create most of the problems. This rule can be applied in many ways. The 80 percent and the 20 percent are only estimates. The good news is that by focusing on the vital few, failures can be better controlled, satisfaction of the most important customers can be increased or 80 percent of the complaints can be eliminated.

- Cause and effect (Ishikawa) diagrams — Often workers spend too much time focusing improvement efforts on the symptoms of problems rather than on the causes. The Ishikawa or fishbone chart is a cause-and-effect diagram that captures all the possible causes of a problem in a format designed to show their relationships to the problem (the effect) and to each other. The diagram resembles the skeleton of a fish (ISM *Glossary* 2014). The diagram shows the problem as the head of the fish, major causes as the ribs of the fish and sub-causes forming smaller bones off the ribs of the fish. The facilitator moves to root causes by systematically asking brainstorming participants the question, "Why?". This is sometimes referred to as the five whys.

- Check sheets — Check sheets are data gathering tools that can be used in forming a histogram. Check sheets can be either tabular or schematic.

- Scatter diagrams — A scatter diagram is a graph used to analyze the relationship between two variables. One variable is plotted on the x-axis and the other on the y-axis. The graph will show possible relationships between them. Regression analysis and other statistical techniques can be used to quantify those relationships (ISM *Glossary* 2014).

- Flowcharts or process maps — A flowchart is a diagram of the steps of a process. Each step is identified in sequence along with its key characteristics, such as time involved (ISM *Glossary* 2014).

- Control charts — These graphs or diagrams are used in statistical process control (SPC) to record, measure and analyze variations in processes to determine whether or not outside influences are causing a process to "go out of control." The objective is to identify and correct such influences to keep the process in control (ISM *Glossary* 2014).

The seven managerial tools for improvement — In addition to the seven basic tools of quality is another set of tools that focus more on group processes and decision-making. These tools are known as the New Tools for Management. These tools have their roots in Japanese practice and date back prior to World War II. The New 7 Tools (N7) were developed by a research effort enacted by a committee of the Japanese Society for QC Technique Development.

- The affinity diagram — When solving a problem, it is often useful to first surface all the issues associated with the problem. A tool to do this is the affinity diagram, which is a total quality management (TQM) tool in which the members of a team each sort data in silence, looking for associations. After sorting, the team identifies the associations found, the critical links and the issues that emerged (ISM *Glossary* 2014).

- The interrelationship digraph — After completing the affinity diagram, it might be useful to better understand the causal relationships between the different issues surfaced. The tool for doing this is the interrelationship digraph.

- Tree diagrams — With the affinity diagram, teams identify key issues relating to a problem. The tree diagram is useful to identify the steps needed to address the given problem.

- Matrix diagram — The matrix diagram is similar in concept to quality function deployment in its use of symbols. As with the other N7 tools, matrix diagrams show the relationship between two, three or four groups of information. It can also give information about the relationship, such as its strength, the roles played by various individuals or measurements.

- Prioritization matrices — These are similar to the analytical hierarchy process developed by Thomas Saaty. When different priorities are obtained from the tree and matrix diagrams, weighted matrices are used to prioritize which variables or topic should be emphasized.

- Process decision program chart — A process decision program chart is a tool used to help brainstorm possible contingencies or problems associated with the implementation of some program or improvement.

- Activity network diagram — The activity network diagram is also known as a PERT diagram and is used in controlling projects. This is known as an Activity on Node Chart (AON).

The N7 tools are useful for managing longer projects that involve teams. With the B7 and N7 tools, the supply management professional has a reasonably good set of skills that will help in managing many projects. It is important to note these tools have been successfully used within many different settings, cultures and education levels. The power of these tools is that with the tools and the PDCA (plan-do-check-act) cycle, organizations have a simple, easy to understand methodology for solving unstructured problems. The tools are especially useful when used in teams. Many of these tools are also fun to use, which is often seen as a plus. By using these tools effectively, unproductive meeting time is reduced to a minimum and good, fact-based decisions are made.

The 5S System is a process improvement method that offers a practical approach to making improvements, whether at the office, logistics function or warehouse. By assigning everything a location, time is not wasted looking for items. It is a concept that originated with the Japanese and has five rules — Seiri (Sort), Seiton (Set in Order), Seiso (Shine), Seiketsu (Standardize), and Shitsuke (Sustain) (ISM *Glossary* 2014). Sorting takes place first, where unused items are separated and thrown away. Set in order — straightening the workplace so items are easy to find — is the second step. Shining is the third step, which means to initially clean the work area and then follow up with a daily cleaning thereafter. The fourth step, standardization, means that standards are set for the workplace and work practices, and the organization and its employees operate in a consistent and standardized fashion. This might include standard paint colors for electrical lines or air hoses, standard labels for temperature gauges, or the way customer service representatives answer the telephone. Also, procedures are standardized. This provides a great basis for ISO 9000 registration. Finally, sustaining — maintaining the changes that have been made as well as continually improving and training on these changes — takes place. The reason the 5Ss are useful to help start quality initiatives is that they help to develop the discipline needed to improve quality. Such discipline requires cultural change that can occur as a result of implementing the 5Ss.

D) **Statistical tools** — Statistical process control (SPC) is a technique using the application of statistical control charts in measuring and analyzing the variation in processing operations. The methodology monitors the process to determine whether outside influences are causing the process to go "out of control." The objective is to identify and correct such influences before defective products are produced, and thus keep the process in control (ISM *Glossary* 2014).

If the process is tightly controlled, then its output (products) will be within allowable tolerance. SPC's primary activities are directed toward the following:

- Defining the process (using tools such as data collection, histograms, run charts and process capability)

- Reducing variation (using tools such as cause-and-effect diagrams, Pareto charts, brainstorming and team-based problem solving).

BIBLIOGRAPHY

American Society for Quality, http://asq.org/learn-about-quality/new-management-planning-tools/overview/matrix-diagram.html, June 27, 2013.

Brassard, M. *The Memory Joggger II*, Goal/QPC, Methuen, MA, 1994.

Cavinato, J.L., A.E. Flynn, M.L. Harding, C.S. Lallatin, M.L. Peck, H.M. Pohlig, S.R. Sturzl and V. Tucker (Eds.). ISM *Glossary of Key Supply Management Terms*, 6th edition, Institute for Supply Management®, Tempe, AZ, 2014.

Foster, S.T. Jr. *Managing Quality: Integrating the Supply Chain*, 5th edition, Prentice Hall, Upper Saddle River, NJ, 2013.

Develop, measure and evaluate quality requirements to continuously improve supplier performance.

To maintain or gain a competitive advantage, supply management professionals are responsible for not only monitoring but also finding ways to improve supplier performance. The process begins with understanding customer or user needs and desires and then balancing that with limitations related to supplier capabilities and the law. Supply management professionals can then develop and implement a plan to assure continuous improvement.

1) Customer/user requirements

When discussing the service component of a manufacturing organization or pure services, it is important to determine customer requirements. This involves service design, data gathering from customers and strategic competitor benchmarking. Customer benefits packages or bundles are methods for identifying and documenting customer requirements. User requirements are usually associated with information technology customers who use systems. Defining user requirements involves interactively working with the customer to develop system specifications, including functionality, user interface design, hardware specifications and performance requirements.

2) Service level agreements (SLAs)

A common term in services purchasing, an SLA defines the scope of work, sets the expectations and defines the relationship of the buyer and service provider. It typically addresses what the provider is promising, how it will perform, the metrics and means of measurement, the consequences in the event of failure to perform, and any longer-term aspects of the agreement. It is commonly used with application service providers (ISM *Glossary* 2014). The sections of an SLA may vary. However, some of the most common elements are:

- Introduction

- Scope of work

- Performance, measurement and feedback

- Conflict management

- Remuneration

- Customer role and responsibilities

- Warranties and remedies

- Intellectual property rights, nondisclosure and security

- Legal responsibility in case a dispute occurs

- Termination

- Signatures, etc.

An SLA will specify expectations and desired service levels, support and incentives. The purpose of the SLA is to specify the customer's expectations, to provide a framework for resolving disputes when they occur and to place bounds on the relationship of the parties in question.

A) **Service (for example, customer satisfaction, lead time, on-time)** — This specifies service levels and requirements. This includes delivery, service design, lead times, expected levels of customer satisfaction and execution.

B) **Cost performance** — This specifies price, service costs and ancillary costs. This may include a differentiation between price and total cost of ownership.

C) **Quality** — Many quality-related factors can be negotiated, such as acceptable quality levels, specifications, requirements relative to statistical quality control, service and product design, service bundles and other factors. Some of these are discussed below.

    1.0 **Periodic inspections** — This often involves periodic or sequential sampling plans. This will involve specification of the types of tests to be performed, sample procedures and handling of defective materials.

        1.1 **Internal requirements** — Before selecting a supplier, supply management professionals should identify internal requirements. The specifics of the requirements depend on the product or service being purchased. Internal requirements can be process-oriented, product-oriented or supply chain-oriented. For example, supply management professionals may specify dimensions, tolerances, delivery expectations, due dates and other items. This documentation is often included in the RFP process.

    2.0 **Customer requirements** — A well-designed SLA establishes both the "as is" business processes and the "to be" processes. The "as is" process sets up the baseline activities for cost and quality (or performance) improvement goals. The supply management professional works closely with the internal stakeholder to develop the acceptable processes and metrics to define the level of work to be performed.

3.0 **Statistical methods/techniques** — These can include, but are not limited to, sampling procedures, acceptance sampling, metrology, measurement technology such as calipers or infrared, use of attributes or variables control charts, process reliability and other technical measurements.

4.0 **Testing methods** — Customers may wish to specify testing methods used including, but not limited to, destructive testing, tests using certain chemicals or measurement devices, certain government required tests or other procedures in manufacturing. Relative to service level agreements, a customer might specify how a software developer will test the software to ensure proper function and compliance to specifications.

5.0 **Levels of inspection** — This refers to the rigor of inspection required for particular aspects of a product or service. Examples of levels of inspection include visual inspection, rigorous visual inspection with requirements or inspection with equipment. These are set as internal targets for inspection to ensure necessary rigor in the inspection process and that inspections are cost-effective.

3) Measurements methods

This section discusses methods for gathering and evaluating data relating to customers and processes.

A) **Customer surveys** — The customer service survey is used by marketers and supply management professionals in determining areas of strength and areas for improvement in quality systems. A survey (or instrument) consists of a series of items (or questions) that are designed to capture perceptions. The number of items is determined by the purpose of the instrument and the willingness of respondents to spend time filling out the survey. A four-step process for developing surveys is as follows:

- Identify customer requirements.

- Develop and validate the instrument.

- Implement the instrument.

- Analyze the results.

B) **Focus groups** — When the understanding of a certain dimension of customer service is incomplete or unclear, and there is no established body of literature in either the research or practitioner journals concerning customer desires or needs, qualitative research methods are useful for learning more about a topic. A qualitative approach many organizations use is the focus group. Groups are focused in two ways. First, focus groups draw individuals with similar characteristics or demographics; second, focus groups narrowly address a single topic or group of topics. This limits the discussion to those market segments and dimensions that are of particular interest to the organization. There are a variety of different approaches to focus groups. At times, the focus groups are run by the organization desiring the information; at other times, consulting agencies or other organizations are asked to perform the focus groups on behalf of the client.

C) **Scorecards** — A very important tool for measuring performance is a balanced scorecard. A balanced scorecard is a performance management system developed by Kaplan and Norton that links performance measures to each other and to the organization's vision and strategy. The key performance categories are financial performance, customer knowledge, internal business processes, and learning and growth (ISM *Glossary* 2014). Balanced scorecards can be created and analyzed using computer software and communicated to management on a regular basis — weekly, monthly, quarterly and annually. The usefulness of the balanced scorecard comes from integrating financial measures of business success such as key metrics with nonfinancial, operational information about the business including customer satisfaction and process performance measures.

D) **Potential distortions (for example, subjectivity of end user, internal training, validity of data)** — There are many ways that data can be distorted or misinterpreted. Therefore, it is important to understand the limitation of any data gathering method. Measurement systems analysis (MSA) is a tool for determining whether variation is a result of actual process variation or simply measurement error. Auditing is typically needed when there is suspicion that suppliers are intentionally misrepresenting data.

E) **Benchmarking** — See Task 2-H-2-2-E for a discussion on benchmarking methods.

F) **Weighted point** — Weighted point is a method of evaluating suppliers for selection or for measuring performance. Supply management professionals establish key performance factors, place a relative weight on each factor (usually a percentage) and rate the supplier on each factor using a predetermined rating scale. Final scores are determined by multiplying the rating by the weight for each factor and then adding up the results for a total score.

G) **Categorical** — This is a method for rating suppliers' performance (either expected or actual) in which specific evaluation criteria are rated according to categories such as plus, neutral and minus.

H) **Cost-ratio** — In evaluating suppliers, it may be helpful to compute performance to cost ratios. Cost-ratio is a method of supplier performance evaluation that measures the costs of quality, delivery and service separately for each supplier. Cost ratios are determined by dividing these costs into the total purchases from each supplier. Competitive bids from these suppliers are then adjusted based on their overall cost ratios.

4) Legal requirements

At times, there are regulatory or legal requirements that must be specified relative to a particular product or service. These legal requirements are often disclosed in the SLA so that compliance can be specified by the provider. Often, these legal requirements are negotiated and specified in contracts or purchase orders. When dealing with international suppliers, language of contracts and differing legal requirements become paramount.

5) Supplier capacity and capabilities

This involves specifying how much capacity will be necessary to perform needed services. This also involves specifying needed capabilities such as product design, supply chain capabilities and quality assurance.

6) Various quality processes

A) **Six Sigma** — Six sigma represents a well thought-out packaging of quality tools and philosophies in an honest effort to provide rigor and repeatability to quality improvement efforts. Six sigma is much more cost reduction-oriented than traditional continuous improvement. Six sigma is organized around creating champions, black belts, green belts and, in some situations, yellow belts. From the early days of improving the robustness of design at Motorola, six sigma has morphed into an organizationwide program for improvement involving hierarchical training, organizational learning and pay-for-learning. At the core of six sigma is the following equation:

$$Y = f(X)$$

Strictly speaking, this means that Y (the dependent variable) is a function of X (an independent variable). To six sigma practitioners, an output is a function of inputs and processes where:

Y = output (key business objectives and measures)

f = function (interrelationships to be controlled and managed)

X = controllable and noncontrollable variables that affect Y

The six sigma process follows the DMAIC procedure. DMAIC stands for Define, Measure, Analyze, Improve and Control.

Six sigma programs include champions (upper managers who champion projects), black belts (quality specialists who have received extensive training) and other team members who are involved in these improvement efforts. For additional information, see Tasks 2–G–1 and 2–G–2.

B) **Lean Six Sigma** — Lean Six Sigma focuses on what the organization's customer considers critical to the quality of its products and services. Using the DMAIC procedure described above, organizations can improve product and service quality. The customer's critical to quality (CTQs) needs should first be defined. Then, a value stream map is drawn to understand the steps involved in each process, identifying any non-value-adding steps, and removing or diminishing these steps and waste. Measurements using accurate data should be taken to analyze processes. Control charts are an effective measurement tool to determine the current state of a process. Solutions can then be developed to make improvements. The next step is implementation of the identified solutions. The process should continue to be monitored through control charts, customer surveys or other measures. Employees are critical to improving processes and should be adequately trained. For additional information, see Task 2-G-2.

C) **ISO** — ISO was discussed in Tasks 2–C–1, 2–D–4 and 2–H–1.

D) **Statistical Process Control (SPC)** — SPC was discussed in Task 2–H–1.

E) **Process capability (Cpk)** — Process capability is defined as a measurement of supplier quality that compares existing processes, constraints in these processes and competitive technologies to upper and lower specification limits to determine if process consistently results in products that meet specifications. Two indices commonly used to measure process capability are Cp and Cpk (ISM *Glossary* 2014).

There are two purposes for performing process capability studies:

- To determine if a process consistently results in products that meet specifications

- To determine if a process is in need of monitoring through the use of permanent process charts.

Process capability studies help process managers understand whether the range over which natural variation of process occurs is the result of the system of common (or random) causes. There are five steps in performing process capability studies. The five steps are outlined below:

1) Select a critical operation. These may be bottlenecks, costly steps of the process, or places in the process where problems have occurred in the past.

2) Take k samples of size *n*, where x is an individual observation:

   - where $19 < k < 26$

   - if x is discrete $n > 50$ (as in the case of a binomial)

   - or if x is a measurement $1 < n < 11$.

   - Note that small sample sizes can lead to erroneous conclusions.

   - Use a trial control chart to see if the process is stable.

   - Use a chi-square goodness of fit test or kurtosis to see if the process is normally distributed.

3) Compare process natural tolerance limits with specification limits.

   Note that natural tolerance limits are three standard deviation limits for the population distribution. This can be compared with the specification limits. As they are from a population distribution and not a sampling distribution, these are not process control limits.

4) To compute process capability indices, compute an upper capability index (C_{pu}), a lower capability index (C_{pl}) and a capability index (C_{pk}). The formulas used to compute these are:

   $C_{pu} = (USL - mean) / 3s$

   $C_{pl} = (mean - LSL) / 3s$

   $C_{pk} = min \{C_{pu}, C_{pl}\}$

   Where: USL = upper specification limit
   LSL = lower specification limit
   mean = computed population process mean
   sigma = population process standard deviation

5) Make a decision concerning whether the process is capable. While different organizations use differing benchmarks, the most common benchmarks for process capability are 1.25, 1.33 and 2.0. For example, processes that achieve capability indexes (Cpk) of 1.25 are capable, of 1.33 are highly capable, and of 2.0 are world-class capable (six sigma).

BIBLIOGRAPHY

Cavinato, J.L., A.E. Flynn and R.G. Kauffman (Eds.), *The Supply Management Handbook*, 7th edition, McGraw-Hill, New York, 2006.

Cavinato, J.L., A.E. Flynn, M.L. Harding, C.S. Lallatin, M.L. Peck, H.M. Pohlig, S.R. Sturzl and V. Tucker (Eds.). ISM *Glossary of Key Supply Management Terms*, 6th edition, Institute for Supply Management®, Tempe, AZ, 2014.

Foster, S.T. Jr. *Managing Quality: Integrating the Supply Chain*, 5th edition, Prentice Hall, Upper Saddle River, NJ, 2013.

Index

A

ABC (activity-based cost) 84, 134

ABC inventory classification system 84, 89, 102

Acceptance sampling 191-4, 205

Action plans 43, 71-2, 128, 134

 corrective 120-1

Advance shipping notices (ASNs) 39

Air transportation 49-50

American National Standards Institute (ANSI) 67

Application service providers 203

Asset classification 101

Asset disposal 105, 107

Asset management 62, 103, 105

Asset recovery 106-7

Asset tags 102-3

Asset tracking 103-4, 106-7

Asset value 106

Assets 14, 70-2, 81, 91, 101-9

   capital 104, 153

   current 101-2

   intangible 101

   non-inventory 114

   organizational 106

Audit 127, 131-4, 182, 184, 189

   external 127, 132, 183

   internal 127, 131-2

Audit processes 127

B

Balance sheet 81-2, 92, 105

Balanced scorecards 119, 206

Bar coding 70, 94, 102-3, 105

Benchmarking 171, 177, 195-6, 206

Bill of materials 92, 114

Bottlenecks 7, 209

Budget 19, 41, 67, 74, 164, 168-9

Business case 161

Business continuity 71

Business control 117-18

Business cycle forecasting models 3, 29

Business cycles 2, 13-14, 17, 21

Business functions 95, 98, 105

Business objectives 102, 117, 123

Business operations 37, 71, 137

Business partners 55, 94

Business plans 30, 117

Business process improvement initiatives 172

Business units 62, 64, 123, 125, 140

C

C-TPAT 55, 94

Capability indexes 209

Capability maturity model integration, see CMMI

Capacity utilization 14, 146

Capital equipment 104

Carriage 53-4

Cash flows, discounted 161

Centralized warehouse system 82

Change management 166

Charts

   flow process 109

   process decision program 199

CMMI (Capability maturity model integration) 173-4, 177

CMMM (Contract management maturity model) 174

Collaborative Planning Forecasting and Replenishment, see CPFR

Commodities 3, 9-11, 13, 24, 75, 83

Compliance 33, 112, 127-8, 132, 134, 188, 205, 207

Conference

   pre-performance 166

   pre-proposal 165

Consumer Price Index 12-13

Contract award strategy 163, 166

Contract management processes 174-5

Control Systems

    continuous review inventory 40, 144

    fixed order interval inventory 144

    fixed-order interval inventory 86

    supply management professional's enterprisewide quality 180

Core competencies 64, 66, 79, 81

Cost/benefit analysis 65, 134

Cost ratios 207

Cost variance 167

Costs

    acquisition 109

    activity 173

    activity-based 134

    additional 5, 58, 62, 90

    ancillary 204

    compromise 38

  estimated 161, 164

  fixed 43, 81

    high 12

    higher 5, 82

    initial 70

    internal 155

    long-term 158

    lower 31, 117, 152

    manpower 38

    marginal 91

    meeting 167

    minimal 77, 141

    minimum 36, 176

    monitor 46

    order 86, 145

    original 91

    overhead 173

    per-unit 158

    picking 82-3

    potential 9, 155

    procurement 7

    stocking 82

    supplier's 167

    target 91, 150, 155

    total 36, 65, 102, 118, 144, 146, 173, 180

    variable 74

CPFR (Collaborative Planning Forecasting and Replenishment) 31-3

CPI 12

Cpk 186, 208-9

Critical path 164

Currencies 16, 140

Cycle counting 80, 88-9, 96, 144

Cycle time 154, 175

D

Damage 46, 50, 57-9, 90-1, 114

Damage claims 57

Damaged inventory 145

Damaged material goods 114

Decentralized warehouse system 82

Decision trees 23

Deferred cost 101

Deflation 14

Deflator, implicit price 10, 12

Delivered at Frontier (DAF) 53-4

Delivered at Place (DAP) 53

Delivered at Terminal (DAT) 53

Delivered Duty Paid (DDP) 54

Delivered Duty Unpaid (DDU) 53

Delivered Ex Quay (DEQ) 53-4

Delphi method 20-1, 24

Depreciation 15, 101-3

DEQ (Delivered Ex Quay) 53-4

Design control 187

Design parameters 141

Design process execution 151

Design products 187

Development costs 61, 154

Diagrams

    activity network 199

    affinity 198-9

Disaster recovery plans 71-2

Disposal 4-5, 55, 91, 105, 108, 110-13

H

Hazardous 55, 75

Histograms 197-8, 200

I

Implementation process, defined 128

Imports 3, 12, 16, 51

In-house, produced 137

Incentives

    developing process improvement 114

    tax 36

Income statement 81

Incoterms® rules 52-5, 57

Indexes 3, 11-12, 14-15, 17

    composite 3, 17

Indicators

    business system 17

    key performance 81, 104, 119

Industrial Production Index 14

Inflation 1, 4, 11, 14, 22, 25, 27, 147

Inspection procedures 185-6

Inspections

    final 181-2, 188, 192

    in-process 188

    incoming 133, 179-81

    visual 205

Interest rates 12, 14, 21, 25

International trade 2-3, 25, 49

Interrelationship digraph 199

Inventory

    additional 5, 145

    consolidating 92

    excess 31, 109-10

    excessive 92, 114

    in-process 35

    managed 31-2, 85

    obsolete 91, 145

    on-hand 40, 114

    organization's 70, 102

    organization's asset 107

    physical 85, 88, 103

    physical asset 104

    replenish 138, 140

    status of 85

    stored 36, 69

    vendor-managed 30-1, 143

Inventory accuracy 70, 74, 85, 87-8, 91, 93-6, 107-8

Inventory classification systems 84, 102

Inventory consolidation 92-3

Inventory control 37, 102, 106, 159, 171, 189

Inventory investment 83, 139

Inventory investment loss 91

Inventory level changes 13, 29

Inventory levels 7, 87, 91, 138, 189

    expected 138

    planned 158

Inventory planning 158

Inventory policies 96, 102

Inventory position 40, 86, 144

Inventory records 70, 85-6, 89-90, 138

    perpetual 76, 144

Inventory system

    perpetual 85

    projected 139

    time-phased computerized 140

Inventory turnovers 42, 74, 189

ISO 55, 66-8, 94, 132, 182-5, 187, 190, 200, 208

Items

    bottleneck 7

    flammable 75

    hazardous 97

    indirect 64

    mishandled 74

    obsolete 88, 108

    reordering 85

    replenishing 31, 143

    reworked 115

    sensitive 71

Services
    design 152
    guaranteed expedited 49
    internal 196
    manufacturing organizations purchase 64
    multiple 42
    outsourced warehousing 80
    support 41
    value-added 79
Shipment, multimodal 50
Shipped products quality level 118
Shortages 24-5, 140
Shrinkage 87, 89
Sigma 161, 175-6, 186, 207, 209
Sigma process analysis 161
SKUs (Stock-keeping unit) 39, 61, 87-8
SLA (Service level agreements) 203-5, 207
SMI (Supplier-managed inventory) 30-1, 85, 143
Software
    asset tracking 103
    inventory management 105
Sorting 199-200
SOW 163-4
Spare parts 112-13
SPC (statistical process control) 179-80, 185-8, 198, 200, 208
Specifications 61, 65, 151, 155, 186, 191, 204-5, 208
SQC, see statistical quality control
Stakeholders 62, 72, 162
Standard deviation 22, 27, 145, 209
Standard output measure 175
Statistical process control, see SPC
Statistical quality control (SQC) 186, 192, 204
Statistics 13, 15, 21-2, 27, 143
Stock count 85
Stock location system 40
Stockouts 5, 31, 73-4, 86, 144

Strength, weaknesses, opportunity, threats (SWOT) 5, 79, 160
Structures
    functional organizational 164
    matrixed organizational 164
    organizational 164
    projectized organizational 165
Supplier assessment 110
Supplier assurance 118
Supplier base 154
Supplier capabilities 203
Supplier capability/capacity analysis 158
Supplier capacity 147, 207
Supplier capacity analysis 147
Supplier certification 179, 187
Supplier certifications/registrations 182
Supplier data 33
Supplier delivery problems 154
Supplier diversity 128-9
Supplier expertise 154
Supplier identification 87
Supplier input 125
Supplier management 187
Supplier optimization 139
Supplier orders 139
Supplier performance 17, 179, 203
Supplier performance evaluation 207
Supplier price index 11
Supplier proposals 29
Supplier quality 208
Supplier quality practices 179
Supplier relationships 184
    well-developed 72
Supplier report cards survey 118
Supplier research 6
Supplier shortages 158
Supplier surveys 118
Supplier transaction index measures 118
Supplier workshops 176

Suppliers
    approved 179-80
    categorize 179
    certified 67, 180, 182
    critical 176
    diverse 129
    diversity 118
    evaluating 206-7
    external 172
    idle 26
    international 9, 93, 207
    key 31, 132, 140, 150, 179
    multiple 72
    preferred 179
    prequalified 180
    primary 179
    recommended 179
    selected 150
    single 144
    small 158
    sustainable 33
    switch 7
    third-party logistics 77
    third-tier 179
Supply chain costs 31
Supply chain management 31, 70, 98-9, 172, 190
Supply forecasts 9, 147
Supply management audit 127
Supply management budgets 13
Supply management components 159, 171
Supply management efficiency measures 118
Supply management performance 123
Supply management plans 165
Supply management policies 127-8
Supply management practices 95
Supply management process 107, 131
Supply management training 128
Sustainability 33

Sustainability initiatives 33
SWOT analysis 79-80, 160
Systems
    communication 137, 142
    decentralized 82
    operating 179, 195
    periodic 86
    perpetual 85-6

T

Tagless systems 69-70
Tariffs 2, 4
Teams
    cross-functional 61, 63, 150
    service design 150-1
Terrorism 25, 38, 55-6, 67, 94
Testing phase 142
Third-party logistics organizations 81
Threats 5-6, 24-5, 55, 79, 160
Time-series analysis 21
Tolerance 96, 186, 200, 204
Tooling 151, 158
TQM (total quality management) 186, 199
Trade
    balance of 16
    free 4
Transportation analysis 46
Transportation costs 5, 52, 77, 82
Transportation modalities 45
Transportation providers 45
Transportation services 81
Tree diagrams 199

U

UCC (Uniform Commercial Code) 54, 181
UID 70, 103
Uniform Commercial Code, see UCC